UNHOLY
ALLEGIANCES
HEEDING REVELATION'S WARNING

UNHOLY
ALLEGIANCES

HEEDING REVELATION'S WARNING

DAVID A. deSILVA

HENDRICKSON
PUBLISHERS

Unholy Allegiances: Heeding Revelation's Warning

ISBN 978-1-61970-141-0

Scripture translations are the author's unless otherwise marked.

Printed in the United States of America

First Printing — November 2013

Library of Congress Cataloging-in-Publication Data

DeSilva, David Arthur.
    Unholy allegiances : heeding revelation's warning / David A. deSilva.
      pages cm
    Includes bibliographical references and index.
    ISBN 978-1-61970-141-0 (alk. paper)
    1. Bible. Revelation—Criticism, interpretation, etc. I. Title.
    BS2825.52.D47 2013
    228'.06—dc23
                2013012854

To the Rev. Dr. Jim Ridgway, Sr., founder,
and Mr. James Ridgway, Jr., president
of Educational Opportunities Tours,

in honor of forty years of facilitating travel
to the lands of the Bible

TABLE OF CONTENTS

LIST OF ILLUSTRATIONS

PREFACE

Many books on Revelation written for a general audience push readers to accept the author's new and innovative decoding of Revelation's "prophecies" in the current world situation. Often this includes some prediction of what the author believes will come to pass in the readers' near future based on his or her alignment of Revelation with current world politics.

I wrote this book for people who are *not* satisfied with this kind of speculative, fanciful, often manipulative approach to Revelation. I wrote this book for those who suspect that Revelation *does* have an important word to speak to the churches today, but also that John's concern is not to provide a playbook for the end times. I also wrote this book for people like those who were captivated by Harold Camping's predictions of the return of Jesus and the rapture of the faithful in May (and then October) of 2011, or by the myriad other "prophecy experts" who make of Revelation a Christian Ouija board for prognosticating the future. Surely it is time to take John's word to John's congregations in Asia Minor more seriously, and to study the book—in Harold Camping's own words after admitting his failure—"even more fervently . . . not to find dates, but to be more faithful in understanding."

My own starting point for reading and interpreting Revelation is to ask what John's word would have meant to, and how it would have challenged, Christians in the seven churches located in the Roman province of Asia Minor in the late first century C.E. On this basis, I would invite readers to ponder how John would analyze and address our contemporary situation, what he would identify as the significant challenges to preserving faithful response and witness, and how he would change our outlook on the major features of our own landscape such that we become more inclined to overcome those challenges.

Primarily, I wrote this book for people like those who populate my own church and who participate together in small groups or Sunday morning Christian education programs. While I am a New Testament scholar by training and profession, my primary goal for my work is to help people in churches, whether ministry staff or laity, listen to Scripture more intently and intentionally, and wrestle with discerning its guidance for the formation of disciples and faith communities. I believe that much popular writing on Revelation has actually hindered people from such genuine listening and wrestling, and so I am particularly passionate about communicating the fruits of scholarly study of Revelation to the people who gather in churches around this book as part of "the Word of the Lord."

If this book is well illustrated, it is in large measure due to the generosity and efforts of a number of individuals who went out of their way to help, for which I am profoundly grateful. Mr. Victor England of Classical Numismatic Group, Inc. and his assistant Ms. Dale Tatro, Ms. Poppy Swann of Numismatica Ars Classica AG, and Dr. Stefan Krmnicek of the Institut für Klassische Archäologie, Tübingen, graciously gave me permission to use the images of coins depicting facets of Roman imperial ideology. Mr. Travis Markel kindly made certain that I had the highest resolution images available from Classical Numismatic Group, and Thomas Zachmann photographed the coins from the numismatic collection at the Institut für Klassische Archäologie. I also wish to acknowledge Mr. Fernando Real, a talented artist from Brazil, whose stunning depiction of the Whore of Babylon appears in these pages. Ms. Marisa Basso of Folhapress helpfully facilitated the process of obtaining permission to use this image. My own photographs were taken during a ten-day visit to the archaeological sites in Ephesus, Smyrna, and Pergamum, supported by a study leave grant from Ashland Theological Seminary.

The material in this volume has its roots in a workshop I created for pastors and laypersons interested in exploring a reading of Revelation grounded in the world of John, its author, and the seven congregations to which John originally sent his collection of oracles and visions. It was further developed in a series of presentations I created for a group traveling under the auspices of Educational Opportunities Tours, Inc. I am grateful to the Rev. Dr. James Ridgway, the founder and past president of that organization, and to his son, Mr. James Ridgway, the current president, for inviting me to accompany the tour group and to present these lectures. Their commitment to provide not only travel services, but also meaningful engagement with the Scriptures and Christian formation as an integral part of their tours, provided the principal venue in which this book took shape. I am also grateful to them for pressing me to make the material as accessible as possible, which planted in my mind the idea of publishing this material for nonspecialists. As in all my writing endeavors, I am also grateful to the administration of Ashland Theological Seminary, whose support of my work is a token of their commitment to educating not only the students who enroll in our degree programs, but also all who are a part of the Christian church.

ABBREVIATIONS

Old Testament

Exod	Exodus
Lev	Leviticus
Num	Numbers
Deut	Deuteronomy
2 Kgs	2 Kings
Ps(s)	Psalm(s)
Prov	Proverbs
Isa	Isaiah
Jer	Jeremiah
Ezek	Ezekiel
Dan	Daniel
Hos	Hosea
Jon	Jonah
Zech	Zechariah

New Testament

Matt	Matthew
Mark	Mark
Luke	Luke
John	John
Acts	Acts
Rom	Romans
1 Cor	1 Corinthians
Gal	Galatians
Eph	Ephesians

1–2 Thes	1–2 Thessalonians
1 Tim	1 Timothy
Heb	Hebrews
1 Pet	1 Peter
1–3 John	1–3 John
Rev	Revelation

Apocrypha

2 Macc	2 Maccabees
4 Macc	4 Maccabees
Sg Three	Song of the Three Young Men
Wis	Wisdom of Solomon

Dead Sea Scrolls

| 1QH | *Thanksgiving Hymns* |
| 1QM | *Milḥamah* or *War Scroll* |

Greek and Latin Works

Aelius Aristides
    Or.   *Orationes*
Dio Cassius
    Hist.   *Historia Romana*
Josephus
    J.W.   *Jewish War*
Tacitus
    Agr.   *Agricola*
    Hist.   *Historiae*
Virgil
    Aen.   *Aeneid*

LCL   Loeb Classical Library

Chapter 1

DEBUNKING POPULAR MYTHS ABOUT REVELATION

I first read Revelation when I was thirteen years of age, after I had read through the four Gospels and Acts. Like most teenagers I suppose I was allergic to feeling that I was being "lectured," and so the epistolary material of the New Testament did not hold such immediate appeal as the narratives. Revelation was gripping. Its fantastic and mysterious images, its cosmic scope, its astounding pronouncements about the stakes involved in keeping or failing to keep its "word"—Revelation was well crafted to sink its hooks into the reader's mind.

As I sought guidance for understanding, and therefore having a chance at keeping, this "word," I noticed that the people whose guidance I sought tended to have one of two reactions, with very little in between. I went first to the rector of the Episcopal church of which I was a member. He was always open to discussing the faith and the Scriptures, and I had found him to be a great encouragement to me. On this occasion, however, he admitted that he had little exposure to the book, and so he took me to the church library, sat me down with the final volume of the old Interpreter's Bible, and essentially wished me luck. Then there was my maternal grandmother's older sister, whom I simply called "Aunt." Though raised Baptist, she had joined the Seventh Day Adventist church and knew exactly what Revelation was about, from beginning to end. She read about it constantly, and my display of interest prompted a steady flow of conversation and sharing of literature over the space of a decade.

In one setting, then, Revelation was beyond the purview even of the professionals. In the other, it was the interpretive key to the whole canon, the focus for study on the part of every active layperson. In both settings, Revelation was a kind of Pandora's box. In the first setting, it wasn't something that one tended to open. While texts from Revelation might occasionally be read as part of the lectionary cycle, these tended to be only from those portions that spoke of the state of the blessed (e.g., Rev 7:9–17 or Rev 21:1–6 on All Saints' Day). But for the most part, the contents of Revelation were kept safely locked away. In the second setting, every church member was a Pandora, eagerly opening the box and allowing its contents to overrun the world around them, chasing the beast in this or that political figure, following the whore to this or that country, seeing the gallop of the four horsemen in this or that series of news briefs.

This has resulted, most unfortunately, in the loss of the witness of John's voice in the churches. Where Revelation is not read and studied regularly, its silence is evident. Where Revelation is avidly consumed as a playbook for the end times (in which the reader is inevitably always living), John's voice is often equally silent, this time muted by the voice of the interpreter who uses Revelation to speak of things about which John had never imagined, and in the process losing sight of those things that John passionately sought to communicate to the church. The latter have largely dominated public discourse about Revelation.

As people get caught up in the imagery of Revelation and try to find answers to these questions, they often fall headlong into some mistakes, forgetting some of the most basic and most important principles of studying the Bible. In regard to Revelation, in particular, I find many popular speakers and writers, and the many more who follow them, to have been led astray by three basic fallacies—three myths, if you will—about Revelation.

Myth #1: Revelation is about *us*

This misconception may spring from a wholesome desire to find the relevance of this book for us. Or perhaps it springs out of that general self-centeredness that most of us never quite get over entirely. We often forget, in our rush to turn to Scripture to hear a word "for us," that all of these texts originally spoke a word "for them," that is, for communities of faith removed from us by at least nineteen centuries, and that we are the secondary beneficiaries of the pastoral guidance initially intended for them.

John gives some cues that should serve to remind us, as attentive readers, that this book is *not* in fact about *us*. In particular, he signals that Revelation is to be read as a letter, specifically a pastoral letter. After an introductory paragraph in which John does not speak in his own voice, but in an impersonal voice comparable to the openings of the writings of other biblical prophecies (compare Rev 1:1–3 with Isa 1:1; Jer 1:1–3), John's own voice sounds out in words that recall the opening of other early Christian letters: "John to the seven churches that are in Asia: Grace to you and peace" (Rev 1:4 NRSV). The standard formula with which letters began ("sender to addressees, greeting") is clearly present. John even uses a modification of the basic "greeting" already familiar from early Christian letters such as those by Paul and Peter—"Grace to you and peace."

One crucial "reading cue," then, is that John writes a letter addressed explicitly to seven real communities of Christians in the Roman province of Asia Minor (now western Turkey). This is reinforced by the divine command that John hears: "Write down what you see into a book, and send it to the seven churches, to Ephesus and to Smyrna and to Pergamum and to Thyatira and to Sardis and to Philadelphia and to Laodicea" (Rev 1:11). [Fig. 1.1 on p. 4.] John therefore intended his letter to be understood by *them*, to shape *their* perceptions of *their* everyday realities, and to motivate a particular response to *their* circumstances. The pervasive use of the number "seven" in Revelation suggests that the seven churches are, in some way, representative of the achievements and challenges facing churches across the Mediterranean in the first century and across the globe now, such that the words addressed to them speak to churches beyond this circle.[1] Nevertheless, these seven churches are seven *real* churches facing particular difficulties and situations, whose response to their world John wanted

---

[1] Regarding each church as representative of the whole church in a particular era grossly caricatures the periods of church history so described. See "Extended note: The seven epochs of church history" in chapter 4. (p. 103).

to affect profoundly. A grounded and responsible reading of Revelation begins with reading it first as we would read Paul's Letters to the Galatians or Philippians or the Letters of the Elder (1–3 John), namely, as a piece of communication that reveals its meaning and message most fully when we immerse ourselves in the contexts and conversations of its ancient audience, when we exercise ourselves to understand it as a pastoral word to *them* in the midst of *their* concerns and circumstances.

Fig. 1.1. The locations of the churches in Roman Asia addressed by John. Courtesy of Rusty Russell, Bible History Online (www.bible-history.com).

Myth #2: What Revelation reveals is *our future*

A second reading cue emerges even earlier in the book, as an anonymous voice declares, "Privileged . . . the one who is reading out loud, and those who are listening to, the words of *this prophecy*, and who are keeping the things written in it" (Rev 1:3; see also 22:7, 10, 18, 19). The contents are presented as

"the words of this prophecy" (Rev 1:3), a term that, for better
or for worse, *we* tend to equate first with prediction, communicating murky oracles looking off into the distant future, as in
the prophecies of Nostradamus that supposedly spoke of events
centuries after the time of the speaker.

This understanding of prophecy as prediction has given
rise to three of the major schools of thought in regard to interpreting Revelation—the historicist, futurist, and preterist
approaches to the book's "prophecies."

The *historicist* approach reads Revelation as a prediction of
events spanning the period between John's own time and the
future, end-time coming again of Jesus and establishing of the
new heavens and new earth. The visions reveal the course of
history in the long in-between, with the interpreter generally
locating himself or herself toward the end of that span.

The *futurist* approach regards Revelation as consisting of
mostly yet-unfulfilled predictions. Some of Revelation may
pertain to events contemporary with its author ("the things
which are," Rev 1:19), but the vast majority of Revelation's
material speaks of the end-time future ("the things which shall
be hereafter," Rev 1:19). Thus while futurist interpreters also
generally view themselves as living near the beginning of the
"last days," they tend to regard most of Revelation's predictions
as still ahead of them. The oracles to the seven churches are
often read as a means of bridging the distance between John
and the present generation, with each congregation representing a broad period in the history of the church. The futurist
reading allows for the highest degree of literalism, for example,
the expectation that a third of earth's trees and grass will perish.
Since this has never actually happened, the historicist reading
must temper the literal sense somehow in order to connect
the sounding of that first trumpet (8:7) with some past event,
while the futurist reading is free to imagine the scene of destruction more literally.

The *preterist* reading gives more weight to John's consis-
tent emphasis that "the time is near" (1:3; 22:10) and that
the visions are imminently relevant (coming to pass *quickly*:
1:1; 3:11; 22:7, 12, 20). Thus this approach reads Revelation's
prophecies as fulfilled in events of the distant past, whether as

a prediction of events from John's time to the establishment of the Christian state under Constantine (with the millennium commencing with the legalization and empowerment of the Christian religion) or even events culminating in the destruction of Jerusalem (represented, in this reading, by Babylon) in 70 C.E., which is equated with the second coming of Christ.

All three approaches are based on the assumption that by "prophecy" John primarily indicates that he is communicating predictions about specific events that will yet unfold at some point in his first audience's future, and that this is the interpretative key to the book. They differ only in terms of the time frame of that fulfillment. But is "prophecy" essentially "prediction"?

To answer this, we turn to the prophetic utterances of the Hebrew Bible and to the phenomenon of prophecy within the New Testament and early Christian worship. While such prophecy could include a predictive element, it was also—and perhaps primarily—a declaration of God's action in the present or an announcement of God's evaluation of the present actions of God's people, diagnosing problems and calling for realignment with God's values. Prophecy is essentially a "word of the Lord" breaking into the situation of the Lord's people who need guidance or encouragement or a call to repentance and recommitment.

"Prophecy" was a regular experience in the worship life of the Pauline churches. The new pouring out of the Holy Spirit upon God's people resulted in a renewal of the possibility of hearing the divine voice given utterance by the Spirit through the mouths of those who were possessed by the Spirit (Rom 12:6; 1 Cor 12:10, 28–29; Eph 4:11). While there are certainly elements of prediction involved in some prophetic utterances (for example, 1 Tim 1:18), the primary element appears to have been "edification," the revelation of a supra-mundane perspective that invited a radical re-orientation to one's circumstances, practices, or pursuits. This certainly emerges from Paul's own understanding of the prophetic gift at work (at its best) in the Corinthian churches (1 Cor 14:3–4, 23–25, 29–31). In John's situation, Jezebel's own activity as a "prophet" involves chiefly "teaching" (Rev 2:20) in regard to the boundaries of acceptable

Christian practice (although, in her case, those boundaries are considerably wider than John would understand them to be).

In Revelation, the seven "letters" to the seven churches are a prime example of early Christian prophecy. They are better labeled the seven "oracles" to the seven churches, for after the command to John to "write" down the oracle, the actual message to the church begins in a manner recollecting the prophetic formula, "Thus says the Lord" (e.g., "These are the words of the Son of God," Rev 2:18). The risen and glorified Lord speaks a word to the churches through the prophet John, affirming their strengths, diagnosing their weaknesses, calling them to faithful action, threatening judgment upon the recalcitrant, and promising favor for the penitent and faithful. In short, they do precisely what so much of the prophetic corpus of the Old Testament sought to do for the communities of Israel and Judah.

Where a prophet speaks of the future, he or she usually limits the prediction to the immediately forthcoming future, not the distant future: "Forty days more, and Nineveh shall be overthrown" (Jon 3:4 NRSV); "There shall be neither dew nor rain these years" (1 Kgs 17:1 NRSV); and the like. John remains within this range, seen in his emphasis on the "imminence" of the confrontations and events he narrates, his conviction that he speaks about "what must soon come to pass" (Rev 22:6; cf. 1:3, 19; 4:1; 22:7, 10, 12, 20).

The modern "prophecy expert" holds that everything presented in the Bible as a forecast of some future event must be fulfilled at some point. If the "prophecies" of Revelation did not match historical events or figures during the first or second century, they must at some point have such a match. This tenet, however, ignores the primary purpose of prophecy, which is not to give hard and fast statements about an unchangeable future, but to evoke faithful response. Jonah proclaimed that "forty days more, and Nineveh shall be overthrown" (Jon 3:4 NRSV). In response to this vision of the future, the city's inhabitants repented and turned to God, with the result that God spared the city (Jon 3:10). Jonah, like the prophecy expert, was still watching "to see what would become of the city" (Jon 4:5 NRSV), and was bitterly disappointed that the prediction was not to be fulfilled. God's purposes for the prophetic word, however, were fulfilled—the repentance of an entire population. Like Jonah's word, Revelation as prophecy seeks mainly to stimulate faithful response among John's audience, not to provide an absolute blueprint for an uncertain future.

Myth #3: Revelation is written in a mysterious code

One of the most basic assertions made about Revelation is that it is written in a coded language—a code, moreover, that modern "prophecy experts" claim that *we* are somehow in a better position to unlock today than the generations that have come before (see myths 1 and 2!). On the contrary, we are in a far less privileged position when it comes to reading Revelation, since the realities with which it interacts—the features of a landscape very familiar to its first audiences—are for us a quite distant and foreign landscape. If we lived in first-century Ephesus or Pergamum, we would not have to wonder what John could be referring to by the cult of a beast or a prostitute riding astride a seven-headed monster. And if a copy of Revelation fell into the hands of a Roman official of even modest intelligence, the subversive intent of its imagery would not be difficult to grasp in the least.

The third reading cue that John gives us is announced in the very first word of his book: *Apokalypsis*, from which we get our word, "Apocalypse." The Greek word means "unveiling," not "cryptic encoding." Revelation was not sent to those seven churches as a mysterious text needing to *be* interpreted: it was sent to *interpret* the world of those readers. To put this another way, the first readers and hearers did not need a special "key" to unlock Revelation; Revelation *was* the key by which they could unlock the real meaning of what was going on around them, and so respond to it faithfully. Revelation "lifted the veil" from prominent features and persons in the audience's landscape, so that those Christians could see things in their world as they "really were" in light of the bigger picture of God's purposes for the world and the larger picture of the great revolt against God, which God would ultimately crush.

John's apocalypse is not unique in Jewish literature. There are many such narratives of experiences of otherworldly journeys and conversations with otherworldly beings (for example, Daniel 7–12, *1 Enoch*, *4 Ezra*, *2 Baruch*, and the *Apocalypse of Abraham*, to name a few). A typical feature of these apocalypses is that they open up windows on the spaces beyond normal, lived experience—for example, the activity of the throne room of God in heaven, or the Abyss or infernal regions where demons or the damned carry on their activities—as well as the times beyond the audience's contemporary situation and beyond "normal" history—for example, angelic rebellions against God in the past or God's interventions to judge and bring human society back into line with God's standards in the near or distant future. Thus apocalypses set an audience's space within the context of a larger, invisible world, and they set the audience's time in the context of a sacred history of God's activity and carefully defined plan. In so doing, they place the present moment and the challenges of the present situation in an interpretive framework, often explicitly evaluating and addressing those challenges and that situation in light of that larger backdrop derived from the sacred tradition.

Revelation spreads before the eyes of the Christians in Asia Minor that larger canopy of space and time that puts their mundane reality, along with its challenges and options, in its "true" light and proper perspective. Their world will look different when seen in the light of the endless worship that surrounds God's throne, the reality and ferocity of God's judgments upon idolaters, and the rewards of faithfulness, and their interests in and responses to their world will be changed as a result. While Revelation may appear, then, to lift the veil from future events, Revelation's ultimate goal is to lift the veil from contemporary actors, events, and options.

This orientation remains quite different from a fourth interpretative approach that has been prominent in the history of interpretation—the "idealist" approach, which could also be called the "spiritual," "allegorical," or even "archetypal" reading. The idealist approach does not read Revelation as primarily a collection of predictions (like the preterist, historicist, and futurist approaches). Rather, it approaches Revelation as a text that uses symbol, vivid imagery, and dramatic action to express transcendent truths that are valid in every generation. It essentially reads Revelation for "timeless truth," communicated symbolically, about the cosmic battle between good and evil or the trials that must be overcome by the human soul. In so doing, however, the idealist approach violates John's own perspective on the message—that it is imminent, and therefore of special *timeliness*, for the congregations to which he writes. In this way, the idealist reading also overlooks the close correlation of Revelation's primary symbols with the politico-economic realities that characterized Roman Asia Minor.

To sum up: (1) As a pastoral letter, Revelation addresses that which is of concern to seven specific congregations that have grown up within the Roman province of Asia Minor in the second half of the first century; (2) As a prophetic word, Revelation announces God's perspective on the character and challenges of those congregations, confirming loyalty to Christ and his covenant where such loyalty appears, rebuking unfaithfulness to the covenant where it appears, and calling for repentance; and (3) As an apocalypse, Revelation sets before the audience the "bigger picture," both in terms of space and time, that illumines and interprets what the Christians see happening around them. It helps them identify the "real" challenges facing them in their situation, orienting them to respond to those challenges in a manner consonant with that "bigger picture."

Reading Revelation as pastoral letter, early Christian prophecy, and apocalypse orients us toward Revelation in a very different way from those who read it as a road map for *our* future or as a countdown to the end. It orients us to a way of reading, moreover, that coheres better with how we read the rest of Scripture, a way of reading that helps us hear more of Revelation's call and challenge to us in our situation apart from the distracting conversation about determining if or when some "countdown" has begun.

This approach to Revelation summons us to immerse ourselves in the situations of the congregations addressed by John so that we can discover (1) what it was that he found to be objectionable in the practices around and within the churches, (2) what he found commendable or objectionable in the churches' responses to the challenges to walking in line with the lord-ship of God and of his Christ, and (3) what he wanted to see communities of disciples do to live even more fully in line with God's purposes and God's call to seek justice and wholeness for all people. This gives us a basis from which to seek to discern what questions and challenges John would pose to us as com-munities of disciples living in the midst of the contemporary social, political, economic, and global orders. Understanding how John brought the resources of Scripture, prayer, and wor-ship to bear on the situations of his congregations gives us direction for our own process of discernment, so that we can move closer to seeing our world from God's point of view and, therefore, to knowing how to respond to its challenges and entanglements in a way that reflects more closely our primary allegiance to the "kingdom of our Lord and of his Christ."

Roman Asia Minor at a glance

Once we take full notice of the fact that Revelation is a letter addressed to seven very real communities of Christians spread throughout the Roman province of Asia in western Turkey, we are free to read it as a piece of communication that reveals its meaning and message most fully when we immerse ourselves in the contexts and conversations of its ancient audience. As we begin to enter into the world of those Christian communities, then, what do we see? What is the everyday context of the lives of those Christians in Ephesus or Pergamum, for example, and what do they see as they walk from their apartments through the downtown spaces of their cities?

Perhaps the first and most obvious thing they would see would be many people who did not share their convictions about God and God's Christ. An often overlooked challenge for early Christians is the bare fact that the vast majority of people around them have little or no place for the God of Israel or his crucified Messiah. They might acknowledge this God as a tribal deity of a particular people within Rome's empire, but certainly not as a deity as important, imposing, or relevant as the Jews had historically made their God out to be. If they acknowledge

Figure 1.2. Bronze sesterce of Hadrian (emperor 117–138 C.E.) with façade of Temple of Diana Ephesia on the reverse. The cult statue is clearly visible in the center. Courtesy of Institut für Klassische Archäologie, Tübingen (Photo: Thomas Zachmann).

Jesus at all, it is probably as an executed revolutionary—a failure at best and a shameful criminal at worst. The lack of confirmation of the Christians' worldview in the attitudes and practices of their neighbors, who lived (probably often happily) without a care for the God of Jesus the Messiah, was undoubtedly a constant invitation to question the correctness of their own convictions that enjoyed so little social reinforcement.

Another prominent facet of the life of their cities, and indeed the corollary of the first, involved the many cult sites of the traditional Greco-Roman and local gods and of the emperors, the representations of Roman imperialism. Ephesus was famous throughout the Mediterranean for its Temple of Artemis, one of the seven wonders, a source of great civic pride and focus of civic identity. [Fig. 1.2; Fig. 1.3a and 1.3b, see p. **49**.] Antipater of Sidon, a notable tourist in the ancient world, speaks of the Temple of Artemis as the crowning sight of all his travels:

> I have seen Babylon's high walls on the top of which is a road for chariots, the statue of Zeus by the Alpheus, the hanging gardens, the colossal statue of Helios, the lofty pyramids, and Mausolus's expansive tomb; but when I saw Artemis's house rising to the clouds, the splendor of those other marvels grew dim, and I exclaimed, "Except for Olympus itself, the Sun never shone on anything so magnificent." (*Greek Anthology* 9.58 LCL)

The dimensions of the temple were staggering: four hundred twenty-five by two hundred twenty-five feet, its roof supported by one hundred twenty-seven columns sixty feet in height, if Pliny the Elder is correct (*Natural History* 36.21.95). The story of Paul's visit to Ephesus in Acts 19 provides some insight into the connections between a famous temple, the tourist economy and related businesses (like the manufacturing of silver replicas of the cult statue of the goddess as souvenirs), and civic pride, and the way in which the proclamation of the Christian gospel collides with these at every level.

The acropolis of Pergamum was studded with prominent cultic sites of the traditional Greek divinities. [Fig. 1.4, see p. 50.] A vast altar dedicated to Zeus, surrounded by columned porches and all sitting upon a raised marble platform, crowned the brow of the hill, overlooking all the territory below. [Figs. 1.5 and 1.6, see pp. 51 & 52.] Just above it on the hill stood a temple to Athena, which overlooked a vast amphitheater carved into the side of the hill. At stage level, halfway down the hill, a temple to Dionysus stood in close proximity to the theater whose productions were often connected with the worship of that god. [Fig. 1.7, see p. 53.] On another slope of the hill sat a large temple sacred to Demeter, with a central altar and stadium seating running along one of its longer sides. [Fig. 1.8 and 1.9, see pp. 54 & 55.]

Alongside temples to traditional gods stood temples and other sacred cult sites dedicated to the goddess *Roma* and to the emperors. In Pergamum, a temple was built to honor *Roma* and Augustus as early as 19 B.C.E. (with construction starting about a decade earlier), winning for that city the title of "temple warden" (*neōkoros*) of the imperial cult. [Fig. 1.10 and 1.11 on p. 14.] In Ephesus, Julius Caesar and *Roma* were worshiped in a sacred enclosure between the odeion and city hall in the "political" district of the city. [Fig. 1.12, see p. 56.] Toward the end of the first century, a magnificent temple was built in honor of Domitian and his family, the Flavian household, upon a partially artificially raised hill. [Fig. 1.13, see p. 57, and 1.14 on p. 15.] This structure dominated upper Ephesus, and finally won that city regional recognition as an imperial "temple warden" as well.

The sight of these temples remains an ever-present invitation into another story—the public story—about the nature of Roman rule. According to John, this public story that

Fig. 1.10. A denarius of Augustus (emperor, 31 B.C.E.–14 C.E.),
showing Pergamum's Temple to Rome and Augustus, completed in
19 B.C.E., on the reverse. The legend *Com Asiae* is an abbreviation
for *Communitas Asiae*, the provincial council of Asia responsible,
among other things, for the promotion of the imperial cult.
Courtesy of Classical Numismatic Group (www.CNGcoins.com).

constantly surrounds his congregations is incompatible with
God's perspective on Roman rule. As this is a critical element
of Revelation's word to the churches, we will give it detailed
attention below. For now, what is most important to recognize
is the fact that early Christians accepted a distinctly minority report in the midst of a population that oriented itself around the
traditional Greco-Roman gods and that located itself within
the story of Roman rule.

The significance of this never impressed itself upon me until
I spent two months in Sri Lanka, where Christians account for

Fig. 1.11. Silver tetradrachm minted in Asia Minor during the reign of
Domitian (emperor, 81–96 C.E.), showing the cult images of the emperor
and the goddess *Roma* inside the Temple to *Roma* and Augustus. *Roma*
is reaching out with her hand to place a victory wreath on Augustus's
head. Courtesy of Classical Numismatic Group (www.CNGcoins.com).

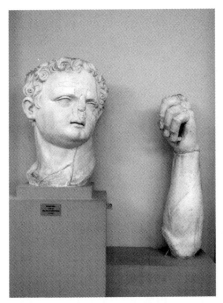

Fig. 1.14. Remains of the Colossal Statue of Domitian from
the Flavian Temple in Ephesus. (Photo: David deSilva)

only seven to eight percent of a deeply religious population. Almost seventy percent would claim to adhere to Buddhism, with perhaps fifteen to sixteen percent following Hinduism, and another seven or eight percent following Islam. For the converts or children of converts to Christianity in that setting, the prominence and pervasiveness of Buddhist statues and shrines in particular, and the visible signs of personal devotion to the Buddha stretching from those shrines to the weaving and purchasing of flower garlands in the marketplace alongside the shops where one buys bread, fruits, and cell phone minutes, serve as a constant reminder of their or their family's departure from the worldview and story held to be true by the vocal majority.

Christians moving from their apartments into the public spaces of Ephesus would also see everywhere the signs of trade and of flourishing economic markets. The harbor at Ephesus, now silted up after centuries of neglect, was once a major port in the eastern Mediterranean with an endless stream of merchandise coming along trade routes from the north and the east to be shipped out to ports closer to the center of the world, and above all to Rome herself. [Fig. 1.15, see p. 58.] This offered the urban Ephesian, and residents of other major cities tied into the network of trade in the province, many opportunities to plug into the local economy or the transportation industry, thus securing one's slice of the Roman pie. Christians in any of these thriving cities would see many families living normal, perhaps even better-than-average lives, and thus would see much that would be desirable for themselves and their own families.

The prosperity promised by Rome, and the possibility of sharing in this prosperity, is a particularly important aspect of the situation of these congregations. The lure of wealth has sunk its hooks quite deep, for example, into the mouths of Laodicean Christians, who can boast of their own prosperity as participants in their local economy while failing to recognize their deep poverty in Christ's eyes, as John sees it. No doubt the hope for economic prosperity also provided the main motivation for developing a theology that could accommodate "eating food sacrificed to idols," something John identifies as a feature of the message of rival prophets in some of the seven churches.

Another important question to ask if we are to enter into the context of the recipients of Revelation and understand the challenges that they face and that John addresses is, What do the Christians' neighbors see when they look at the Christians in their midst? They would see Christians, ironically perhaps, as "atheists," people who failed to acknowledge the existence of the gods of their neighbors and, in the vast majority of cases, the gods of their own ancestors. Here in their midst was a group of people who used to give the gods their due, but who now have turned their backs upon proper piety, both in public and in private, and who speak of their neighbors' and families' gods as sticks and stones. Christians, like the members of other groups nurtured within Judaism, did not merely devote themselves to a particular deity, but also claimed that no other deity existed alongside the One. Such a position was labeled "impiety" (Aelius Aristides, *Or.* 46.309) or "atheism," the specific charge on which the emperor Domitian executed or banished several high-ranking Roman converts to Judaism (Dio Cassius, *Hist.* 67.14.1–3).

The Christians' neighbors, who depended upon the stability now maintained by the empire, saw potential enemies of the Roman peace. Christians were, after all, followers of a man whom a Roman procurator had duly executed for sedition. A central focus in the proclamation of their leaders was some future day when this executed leader would return to bring Roman power to an end in favor of some "kingdom of God," an upheaval that would not be welcomed by (or favorable to) the majority. In short, they would see *formerly* decent citizens or children of decent citizens who have gotten into some very bad company by being lured into this foreign superstition.

In this setting of opportunity and tension, of trying to hold onto the Christian hope without letting go of too much of this world's life, what pressures would we find Christians experiencing? Here Revelation is, as a pastoral word to these believers, our primary evidence for these pressures, since John, giving voice to the diagnoses of the glorified Jesus, explicitly brings these pressures to expression. Other New Testament texts, however, also bear witness to these same pressures being widely experienced by Christians throughout the eastern Roman Empire in some form or other.

First, they no doubt feel the drive within themselves to get a piece of the action, to blend in and thus to drink in the benefits of participating in their city's life and economy. This would require some level of integration into their city's and their associates' religious practice—that is, into the acknowledgement of idols and worship of the traditional gods. There are local preachers and prophets in Pergamum and Thyatira who seek to help make this work theologically for them, so they can hold onto Christ and live prosperous lives at the same time.

> "You have some there who hold to the teaching of Balaam, who taught Balak to put a stumbling block before the people of Israel, so that they would eat food sacrificed to idols and practice fornication." (Rev 2:14 NRSV)

> "I have this against you: you tolerate that woman Jezebel, who calls herself a prophet and is teaching and beguiling my servants to practice fornication and to eat food sacrificed to idols." (Rev 2:20 NRSV)

Christians in some communities feel the pressure brought down by local synagogues, whose members had never been thrilled with this Jewish heresy that seemed to spring up everywhere, and who had every reason since the dismal failure of the First Jewish Revolt to publicly distance themselves from anything with a revolutionary flavor.

> "I know your affliction . . . I know the slander on the part of those who say that they are Jews and are not, but are a synagogue of Satan." (Rev 2:9 NRSV)

> "I will make those of the synagogue of Satan who say that they are Jews and are not, but are lying—I will make them come and bow down before your feet, and they will learn that I have loved you." (Rev 3:9 NRSV)

Many feel pressure from their neighbors, who do not approve of the Christians' anti-witness questioning their much-beloved realities, for example, the existence and favor of the gods or the promise of endless peace and prosperity under Roman rule. These locals even went so far as to lynch a Christian in Pergamum—and John's audiences would all remember from reports told about Nero's Rome what happened to Christians when the beast *really* rears its ugly heads.

> "I also know that you are enduring patiently and bearing up for the sake of my name, and that you have not grown weary." (Rev 2:3 NRSV)

> "You did not deny your faith in me even in the days of Antipas my witness, my faithful one, who was killed among you, where Satan lives." (Rev 2:13 NRSV)

But John is also particularly interested in the complete *lack* of pressure that some believers encounter, or, perhaps better, the fact that some believers encounter exactly and only the *same* pressures that their non-Christian neighbors encounter, because their lives are no different. The Christians in Sardis and Laodicea seem to pose a serious problem for John precisely because they are so *untroubled* by what is going on around them and have become so much a part of it.

> "I know your works; you have a name of being alive, but you are dead. . . . I have not found your works complete in the sight of

my God. . . . Yet you have still a *few* persons in Sardis who have not soiled their clothes." (Rev 3:1–4 NRSV)

"I know your works; you are neither cold nor hot. I wish that you were either cold or hot. So, because you are lukewarm, and neither cold nor hot, I am about to spit you out of my mouth." (Rev 3:15–16 NRSV)

John addresses all of these realities in Revelation, and not merely on their own terms, but under a particular lens—the lens of the larger story, the sacred story, of which they are a part. This story needs such strong reinforcement that John must address his readers not just with a pastoral letter, nor just with prophetic oracles, but with an apocalypse—a revelation of the truth of that larger story.

Questions for Reflection and Discussion: *What approaches to Revelation described in this chapter have you encountered prior to this study? What attracts you to one or more of these approaches? What concerns or disturbs you about one or more of these approaches? What strengths and what limitations do you see in the approach taken in this book?*

Chapter 2

DIVINE EMPEROR, ETERNAL ROME: THE PUBLIC STORY ABOUT ROMAN IMPERIALISM

The members of the churches John addresses are exposed to two very different stories about the "way things are," the "way the world works," and therefore "the way to get along" to their advantage. Inscriptions throughout the city, the coins with which all business was transacted, statues, temples, civic processions, public announcements—all the available media of the first century—tell the first, public story and keep its picture of the "way things are" visible. John tells a very different story, drawing a very different picture—the view from the throne of God and the Lamb—in order to motivate members of seven congregations to resolve the challenges facing them in the way that nurtures a clear, uncompromising witness to that God and his Anointed. Here we will explore the public story in depth, for it is the story foundational to the society and structures in which the members of the seven churches live, and the story that John most directly challenges in his revelation of the way things *really* are in the sight of the One God.

The official narrative about Rome

The public story of Rome begins with the fall of Troy, from whose ashes emerges a hero, Aeneas, who would plant the seeds of a world empire. His story is told by Virgil, a poet in Augustus's court and author of the *Aeneid*, the court epic of the Augustan age. Virgil celebrates the promise of Zeus, the king of the gods, that the Romans would "rule the sea and all the lands about it" (*Aen.* 1.236–237). The poet refers here to

Fig. 2.1. Marcus Agrippa's Map of the World. This modern reconstruction of Agrippa's map from 20 C.E. (known only through descriptions) well illustrates why the inhabited world was spoken of as the *orbis terrarum*, the "circle of lands." Courtesy of www.cartographic-images.net.

the *orbis terrarum*, the "circle of the lands" about the Mediterranean that was considered the civilized world. The map developed under the direction of Marcus Vipsanius Agrippa, Augustus's right-hand man during his war against Marc Antony and consolidation of power, illustrates this concept. The Mediterranean Sea stands at the center of the map, with all the known territories of Europe, Africa, and Asia (as far as India and Sri Lanka) arranged around the Mediterranean in a great circle with a small opening between Spain and North Africa.[1] [Fig. 2.1.]

This was the "world" that counted. Zeus asserts that the destiny of Rome will be to "bring the whole world under law's

---

[1] While no copies of the map itself have survived, it appears to have been the basis for the description of the world found in Pliny, *Natural History* 6.39, written before 69 C.E.

dominion" (*Aen.* 4.232). Indeed, as the wings of the Roman eagle overshadowed more and more of the Mediterranean basin, it exercised "authority over every tribe and people and language and nation" (Rev 13:7). Minucius Felix, a second-century Christian, would write of the Romans that "their power and authority has occupied the circuit of the whole world," referring once again to the concept of the *orbis terrarium.* "Thus it has propagated its empire beyond the paths of the sun, and the bounds of the ocean itself" (*Octavius* 6). Rome was thus indeed seen as "the great city that rules over the kings of the earth" (Rev 17:18 NRSV). These writers were aware that other nations existed that were not under Roman dominion—at least, not *yet*—and that, indeed, often posed a threat to Rome's dominion in some areas and to Rome's borders. Nevertheless, "authority over the kings of the earth" and over "the whole world" was regularly attributed to Rome during this period.

Plutarch, a near-contemporary of John, celebrated the rise of Rome, uniting the Mediterranean region: "Rome developed and grew strong, and attached to herself not only nations and peoples but foreign kingdoms beyond the sea; and then at last the world found stability and security, when the controlling power entered into a single, unwavering cycle and world order of peace" ("On the Fortune of the Romans" 2 [*Moralia* 317] LCL). The gifts and graces of Rome were, according to Virgil, "To pacify, to impose the rule of law, to spare the conquered, and battle down the proud" (*Aen.* 6.851–853).

The power of Rome was visually portrayed in the image of the goddess *Roma*, the visible representation of the "order," the "rule of law," the "peace" and "stability" that Rome's imperial rule brought. She was often featured on the reverse of coins; she is more prominently visible in the cult statues throughout the Mediterranean. [Fig. 2.2, see p. 59.] *Roma* was given the epithet *Aeterna*, an epithet that persists to this day when we hear Rome called "the Eternal City." Thus Rome's supporters and propagandists advanced the bold claim that Rome's destiny was unchanging and everlasting. Plutarch reflects this when he affirms that Rome provided a "secure mooring cable" for the world and used adjectives such as "unwavering" to describe her rule, forgetting all the lessons of world history. [Fig. 2.3a, see

p. 59.] The "prophecy expert" that insists on looking to the future for a beast and his "one-world empire" would do well to look more closely at the images projected of Rome in the first century, and the perception of the Roman Empire held by most of its inhabitants (including John and his audience), and purposefully promoted by imperial propaganda.

Rome was also celebrated as the source of prosperity for the whole world. The luxury of Rome was taken as a sign that a golden age of prosperity had returned to the entire Mediterranean world. In a speech praising Rome, Aelius Aristides, a near-contemporary of John, describes the scene in Rome thus:

> Around lie the continents far and wide, pouring an endless flow of goods to Rome. There is brought from every land and sea whatever is brought forth by the seasons and is produced by all countries, rivers, lakes, and the skills of Greeks and foreigners. . . . Anyone who wants to behold all these products must either journey through the whole world to see them or else come to this city. . . . One can see so many cargoes from India or if you wish from Arabia . . . that one may surmise that the trees there have been left permanently bare, and that those people must come here . . . whenever they need anything! (*To Rome* 11–13 LCL)

Aristides seems to be oblivious to the obvious downside of the Roman economy, but he is a member of the elite and hence a voice for the public, official story of Rome. Such elite sources paint a picture of a world power that brought tremendous benefits to humankind: an end to civil strife, protection from invasion, improvement of means of travel by land (through expert road construction) and by sea (through expansion of ports and harbors), as well as the dramatic reduction of brigandage and piracy. Trade is facilitated, steady distribution of grain and relief in times of shortfall improved, and the rule of law maintained. Much of this is true. Moreover, individual emperors gave significant benefits to cities in Asia Minor, reinforcing the "public discourse" with tangible demonstrations of its truth. Tiberius provided financial assistance to rebuild several cities in Asia Minor after an earthquake in 17 C.E. Nero dredged the harbor of Ephesus, restoring the city's most important economic asset. Domitian provided Laodicea with a stadium and Smyrna with an aqueduct. Rome *could* be a great safety net and a source of significant blessings.

According to this public story, Divine Providence was at work in the rise and reign of Rome, and it was particularly at work in the rise and reign of Augustus and his successors. Rome was an empire long before Augustus, in the sense that the Roman Republic already controlled most of the lands around the Mediterranean. But the Republic offered power-hungry senators (like Marcus Licinius Crassus, Sextus Pompeius, and Julius Caesar) too much opportunity for factionalism and, ultimately, civil war. The Mediterranean was twice subjected to all the horrors of civil war prior to 31 B.C.E., when Octavian, soon to be given the name "Augustus," finally emerged from the strife victorious. He quickly forgave the armies of his rival, Marc Antony, uniting their power to his own.

"By universal consent," Augustus accepted perpetual powers in the republic. Thus government became stable and the provinces flourished again. The phrase "by universal consent" was vital to promoting Augustus's rule as legitimate in the early empire. Toward the end of his life, Augustus drew up a list of his political and military actions and achievements on behalf of the Roman order—the *Res Gestae Augusti*. After his death, this list was inscribed in public spaces across the empire, reminding people everywhere of the legitimacy of the new order ushered in by Augustus and continued now by his successor, Tiberius. In this list, he speaks of "having obtained all things *by universal consent*," and of being given the title "'Augustus' *by universal decree*." Far from being a tyrant, this inscription claims, Augustus had greatness thrust upon him by universal acclaim, and appropriately so, given all he had done on behalf of the world.

Reinforcing the public story

A particularly important expression for naming Augustus's greatest gift and for summing up all of his gifts was the *Pax Augusta*, the Augustan Peace or "Peace of Augustus." This was the beginning of the "Roman peace" (*Pax Romana*) to which reference would be made throughout the principate. It celebrated the end of the series of civil wars, as well as the new ordering of the government throughout the provinces of the empire. The senate commemorated this in an extraordinary way. As Augustus relates in his own words,

> On my return from Spain and Gaul [that is, in 13 B.C.E.], . . . after successfully arranging affairs in those provinces, the senate resolved that an altar of the Augustan Peace should be consecrated next to the Campus Martius in honor of my return, and ordered that the magistrates and priests and Vestal Virgins should perform an annual sacrifice there. (*Res Gestae Divi Augustus* 2.2)

This altar, which has been uncovered and fully restored, is housed within a marble monument of about forty feet square into which is built a staircase leading up to the altar proper. It sat in a prominent location on the Flaminian Way, a major road running through Rome. An obelisk brought back from Egypt as part of the spoils of Augustus's defeat of Cleopatra and Antony was situated in the vicinity such that, on Augustus's birthday (September 23), the shadow of the obelisk would point to the Altar of Peace that celebrated Augustus's victory. This monument, of course, was given empire-wide notice through display on the reverse of several coin mintings. [Fig. 2.3b, see p. 59.] This was just one manifestation of an empire's acclamation of Augustus as the bringer of peace and, with it, the promise of a new era.

An inscription at Priene, another city in Asia Minor between Ephesus and Miletus, captures the spirit of this new age. The provincial council, which was the regional body responsible for the promotion of "the imperial cult," issued a decree that the birthday of Augustus would become the official "New Year's Day" of the calendar year,

> because Providence . . . has set all things in most perfect order by giving us Augustus, whom she filled with virtue that he might benefit humankind, sending him as a savior [*sōtēra*], both for us and for our descendants, that he might end war and arrange all things well, and because he, Caesar, by his appearing [*epiphaneis*], [. . .] surpassed all previous benefactors and leaves posterity no hope of another surpassing what he has done, and because the birthday of the god Augustus was the beginning of the good news [*euangelion*] for the world that came by reason of him.

Speaking of a "savior's" birth as the "beginning of the good news" for the world should cause readers of the New Testament to take notice.[2] The word from the inscription translated as "good news" here is a form of *euangelion*, the same Greek word that is so prominent in the New Testament (whether translated as "good news" or "gospel"). This inscription lauded Augustus as Providence's provision for the "highest good" of the people, a ruler whom Providence "filled with excellence for the benefit of humanity." It hailed him as "savior," one whose gifts to humankind no one would ever surpass in the future. The text of this resolution was inscribed in temples to Caesar across the province of Asia, making its language available to the citizens of the seven cities. Similar acclamations of the reigning emperor reverberate to the very end of the first century C.E. Concerning Domitian, Statius writes: "Behold! He is a god! At Jupiter's command he rules the happy world on his behalf" (*Vita Domitiani* 4.3.128–129). By the standards of Christian language, acclamations of the emperor were no less than messianic.

Temples were erected to Augustus across the eastern Mediterranean, where people were accustomed to treating their rulers and exceptional benefactors as gods. Nicolaus of Damascus, a friend of Herod the Great, explained the phenomenon in the opening of his *Life of Augustus* in this way: "all people address him [as Augustus] in accordance with their estimation of his honor, revering him with temples and sacrifices across islands and continents, organized in cities and provinces, matching the greatness of his virtue and repaying his benefactions towards them." Since the emperor's gifts matched those of the deities, it was deemed only fitting that the expressions of the gratitude and loyalty of his subjects should take on the forms used to communicate with the gods themselves.

Roman power was represented in the seven cities named by John in many ways, but perhaps the most prominent and

---

[2] When Luke speaks of the birth of Jesus as the "good news" concerning the appearing of a "savior" who will benefit "all people" (Luke 2:10–11)—a story in which Augustus appears offstage merely as the person drawing up a list to make sure he can get everyone's money—his readers would have understood the political implications of his proclamation of Jesus's place in the divine scheme of things.

enduring was the imperial cult, the temples, shrines, altars, and cult images dedicated to Augustus and to the members of his household, including those who succeeded to the imperial office. By the end of the first century C.E., thirty-five cities in Asia Minor held the honorific title of "temple warden" (*neōkoros*) of an imperial cult site. All seven cities addressed by John had cultic sites: six (all but Thyatira) had imperial temples; five (all but Philadelphia and Laodicea) had imperial altars and subsidized priesthoods. Pergamum was a center for the imperial cult in the province, the first in the province to honor Augustus with a temple built to him and to *Roma*, authorized in 29 B.C.E., for which it won the honorific title *neōkoros* from the emperor. In the same year, Ephesus rededicated part of its famous Temple of Artemis to the deified Julius and *Roma*.

The connection between imperial cult and civic pride shows up toward the end of the first century and beginning of the second as we find these two cities competing with one another over the title of *neōkoros* of an imperial temple. After Pergamum had held this distinction for over a century, Ephesus undertook a new initiative: the Flavian Temple in the heart of downtown, honoring the living emperor, Domitian, with a colossal statue and cult, erected close by an older temple to Rome and Julius Caesar and the portico dedicated to Artemis, Augustus, and Tiberius. For this display of loyalty and investment in the emperor's rule, Ephesus was finally awarded the title *neōkoros* as well, which it proudly displayed in inscription after inscription. [Fig. 2.4, see p. 60.]

The Pergamenes, of course, were not to be outdone. They still claimed preeminence by virtue of having been the *first* to be named *neōkoros*, and began describing their city thus in inscriptions. [Fig. 2.5, see p. 60.] Fifteen years later, they would win the honor of building the massive temple to Trajan (98–117 C.E.), for which they were awarded the title *neōkoros* a second time, hence they celebrated their civic identity as *dis neōkoros* ("twice awarded temple guardianship") in their inscriptions. [Fig. 2.6a, see p. 61, and 2.6b, see p. 61.] Ephesus would stay in the running, however, winning the honor of building a temple to Trajan's successor Hadrian (117–138 C.E.), thus becoming themselves *dis neōkoros*. Pergamum's response? They began to describe themselves as "first to be twice *neōkoros.*" [Fig. 2.7, see p. 62.]

The cities of Asia Minor were as enthusiastic and as invested in hosting the imperial cult as modern cities are about convincing a major football team to relocate or winning the bid to host the Olympics. This tells us something else about the cult of the emperors. This cult was *not* imposed on the provinces by the emperors; it was locally motivated, the response of provincial populations to the tremendous power of the emperor, which was perceived as truly god-like, and to the benefits that the rule of the emperor brought to the provinces. Such displays of loyalty and gratitude ensured both that the empire would remain strong (hence averting the disasters of civil war and foreign invasion, and ensuring continued peace and prosperity) and that the emperor would remain well disposed toward the province when it was in need of imperial aid. It was a most politic decision that the province's ambassadors to the emperor should also be those elites who held priesthoods in the imperial cult. The beneficent god in the temple was the face of the emperor that Rome wanted the provinces to see; the devoted and grateful functionaries presiding in those temples was the face of the province that Asia Minor wanted Rome to see.

The imperial cult was embedded in the cults of the traditional Greco-Roman gods. Frequently, the statues of the emperor and the Olympian gods shared the same sacred space, emphasizing their connectedness. In Ephesus, for example, we find Julius and Artemis worshiped in the same temple, with a portion of the great Artemision dedicated to the imperial cult. In Pergamum, the Temple of Trajan sits in close proximity to the Temple of Athena and the great altar of Zeus, and overlooks the Temple of Dionysus beside the amphitheatre, where tragedies were performed as part of festivals honoring that god. The emperor was not simply a god, but also the vessel by which the traditional gods established order and showered their gifts upon humanity. As the chief priest of the Roman world (*Pontifex Maximus*), he stood as mediator between the gods and the human race. Many coins minted during the first century provide a graphic depiction of this: on the front ("obverse"), a portrait of the emperor with his titles (including *divi filius*, "son of the deified," and *Pontifex Maximus*); on the reverse, a portrait of some deity, showing that his rule was grounded in the rule of the gods (or of "Fortune," or destiny). [Fig. 2.8, see p. 62.] He ruled by divine right, and his achievements were signs of divine favor.

The emperor was often worshiped in tandem with the goddess *Roma*, or *Roma Aeterna*, the personified and deified representation of Rome. The worship of *Roma* as a goddess was the ultimate legitimation of Roman power and the means by which it operated. Smyrna established a temple to "Rome" as early as 195 B.C.E.. Augustus refused to allow any temple to be consecrated to himself, unless *Roma* were also included. The imperial cult thus also reinforced the belief that Rome was chosen by the gods to rule the world, to subdue all nations and lead them into a golden age of lasting peace and well-being, united under her banner.

Participation in the cults of the emperor and *Roma* demonstrated, in the eyes of the local citizens and elites, appropriate gratitude to the emperor and the Roman order for maintaining the peaceful conditions that facilitated stability, even prosperity. It evidenced the piety and sense of duty that assured one's neighbors of one's commitment to do one's part to support that order on which the well-being of the local community depended. By promoting withdrawal and distance from the cult, Christians fell under their neighbors' suspicion. Christian communities could look like pockets of dissent and, potentially, sedition—at the very least, unreliable members of the community.

Repairing the public story

One more history lesson is necessary to finish setting the stage. The line of succession founded by Augustus remained fairly strong for a century (31 B.C.E.–68 C.E.), but came to a crashing end when Nero committed suicide without leaving a viable heir. The empire reverted once more to chaos in the midst of civil war. 68–69 C.E. is remembered as "the year of the four emperors," each of the first three contenders enjoying their overlapping "reigns" for just a few months each. The

Figure 2.9. Sesterce of Vespasian (emperor, 69–79 C.E.) with reverse depicting Rome being lifted up from the ground (*Roma Resurges*) after the conclusion of the yearlong civil war that brought it to its knees. Courtesy of Numismatica Ars Classica AG (auction 25, lot 410).

armies of the various contenders swept across the Mediterranean from Spain to Egypt, wreaking havoc in every place. This was also the period in which Judea and Jerusalem had been under siege with the suppression of the First Jewish Revolt against Rome. When the fourth contender, Flavius Vespasianus, emerged the last man standing at the end of this year, everyone was prepared to embrace him, along with his two sons, as the ruler of the world. The mortal wound that threatened to dissolve the empire had found healing at last. Rome was able to stand upright once more. [Fig. 2.9.] The cities of Asia Minor had displayed uncommon enthusiasm for the cult of the emperors since Augustus, but this enthusiasm was dramatically renewed. The dedication of the new temple to the Flavian dynasty in Ephesus, eventually to sport a twenty-foot cult statue of the emperor Domitian, bears witness to local fervor.

But the imperial cult was not merely a matter of stone temples, lifeless statues, and voiceless inscriptions passively waiting to be noticed. Priests and celebrants regularly brought these sites and their ideology to life, following a calendar of imperial celebrations, including the monthly commemoration of the reigning emperor's birthday. Leonard Thompson, a contemporary Revelation scholar, describes the scenes thus:

> Imperial temples and sanctuaries were wreathed with flowers. Animals were sacrificed at various altars throughout the main locations of the city, for example, the council house, temples of other deities, theatres, the main squares, stadiums, and gymnasiums. These political, religious, and public buildings were linked together by processions and dignitaries, garlanded animals being

led to slaughter, and bearers of icons and symbols of the emperor. As the procession passed by, householders would sacrifice on small altars outside their homes. The whole city thus had opportunity to join in the celebration.[3]

The air would be filled with the sound of hymns chanted to the emperor and to the gods on behalf of the emperor, as by a community choir formed in Pergamum specifically to sing hymns to Augustus as to a god in the imperial temple. Scenes of worship centered upon the image of the emperor were both elaborate and commonplace in the experience of John and his audience.

Every glimpse of such an edifice or image, every civic festival celebrating the birthday of an emperor or a member of his household, every time a person stopped to count his change—these experiences all extended invitations to the residents of these cities to remember at least a part of this official story about Roman rule: the gods in their generosity gave us Rome and her emperors to provide the gifts of stability, prosperity, safety from harm, relief in need. Thanks be to the gods.

John's references to the public story

When John speaks, then, of a "great city" sitting "upon seven hills" and having "authority over the kings of the earth" (17:9, 17), he speaks of a reality that resonates immediately with the hearers' experience. The seven hills of Rome were, of course, celebrated in literature and coinage. [Fig. 2.10.] A yearly festival in the capital commemorated Rome's expansion to enclose the seven hills within the city limits. On this basis, both Christian hearers and outsiders would immediately connect Babylon with Rome. When John speaks of a city into which the wealth of the world flowed, one would not have to be a Christian to make the obvious connection. And what an extreme makeover *Roma Aeterna* receives at John's hands!

Similarly, when John uses images from Daniel representing world empires to speak of a "beast" (Rev 13:1–2; see Dan

---

[3]L. L. Thompson, *The Book of Revelation: Apocalypse and Empire* (New York: Oxford University Press, 1990), 162.

Fig. 2.10. Sesterce of Vespasian, with the goddess *Roma* seated and reclining on Rome's seven hills. She holds a scepter as a symbol of her authority. A representation of the river Tiber as a god reclines at her feet. Courtesy of Numismatica Ars Classica AG (auction 54, lot 361).

7:3–7), fatally wounded but healed (Rev 13:3), worshiped by "the inhabitants of the earth" in a manner involving a cult image (Rev 13:4, 8, 14), and exercising authority over a multi-ethnic, multi-lingual, multi-national empire (Rev 13:7), the Roman emperors were immediately available to John's hearers as plausible referents, whose cult was practiced in every one of their cities and whose rule and divinity were everywhere proclaimed.

John selected these landmarks from the landscape of first-century Roman Asia for special examination through his apocalyptic lens. Roman imperialism, with its seductive economy and blasphemous imperial cult, is a primary challenge to Christian faith and witness, as John identifies these challenges in Revelation 4–22. John raises his voice alongside those of other protestors like the authors of *4 Ezra* and *2 Baruch*. John was not a solitary, raving lunatic. The asylum was full of people who just couldn't "see things" in line with the official picture that we have been exploring. The multiplicity of voices calling out against Rome's injustices at the close of the first century, of which John's voice was one, helps us see that Jews and Christians in Asia Minor were not only concerned about local affairs, false teachers, or throwing stones at the church or synagogue across the street. The whole Roman imperial system, together with all its local manifestations, was also a major problem. And, in keeping with the claims made previously about the relevance of Revelation for its first audiences, the Christians in Roman

Asia Minor did not have to look beyond their own cities to see what John was talking about, and to understand Revelation as a radical unmasking of the world around them, with all of its challenges and its temptations.

Optional Exercise: Read through the book of Revelation with these realities in your mind. Put yourself in the place of a Christian in Ephesus or Pergamum, to the extent possible. Surround yourself in your mind with the temples to the traditional gods and to the various emperors, with the neighbors who are happy to include the acknowledgement of these gods at their private and public meals, in their business meetings, and in civic festivals. Surround yourself with the bustling activity of tradesmen and merchants and merchant marines loading their cargoes and growing wealthy from trade. Remember Antipas, whose life was forfeited because of his witness against these things. How does John make you look at your world differently? What questions and issues does John raise in regard to what is going on all around you? What does it mean for eternity to get in bed with Rome and its imperialism now?

Chapter 3

THE TRUE CENTER AND THE UNHOLY SCAM: JOHN'S BIBLICAL CRITIQUE OF THE PUBLIC STORY

In the previous chapter, we looked in depth at the "public" story that sought to render Rome's worldwide domination legitimate, an expression of the gods' providential care, a pillar for the stability and security of all peoples, tribes, nations, and languages. In this chapter, we will look at the alternative story—the very different story—that John tells, and the ways in which he works the major players of the story of Rome—the emperors, the local supporters of Roman power, and the figure of *Roma* herself—into that larger story.

The larger story, of course, is the story of the One God, the Creator of heaven and earth, and his past and future interventions in human history. John's story is the story of the Scriptures. He has grounded himself so fully and fervently in the traditional revelations about God, God's character, and God's vision for human community that he speaks from beginning to end in the idiom and images of the Scriptures. He cannot help but see the world through the lens of that tradition, and his Revelation extends an invitation to the churches in Asia Minor to see their local setting and their world through the lens of the scriptural revelation of God as well—to see their landscape anew in the light of God and of the Lamb.

What, then, does Roman Asia and the larger Roman world look like under the light of the sacred tradition and the light of the character of the God who created all that is and is coming in judgment upon all that is?

Fig. 3.1. Gustave Doré's visualization of the throne of God, surrounded by countless, circling throngs of angels (illustration for Dante's *Paradiso*, Canto 31 http://comonns.wikimedia.org/wiki/File:Paradiso_Canto_31.jpg).

Finding the true center

To answer this, we need to start where John does, which is not with things earthly, but with things heavenly. For the focal point of the cosmos, the center from which all things are to be measured, is not in Ephesus or Pergamum, where our congregations live and move and go about their daily business. Nor is the center of the cosmos in Rome, where the great power brokers and shapers of the political scene wield their influence, but in the realm beyond ours.

John's visions begin at the center of John's universe, at the very throne of God (4:2). The way John unfolds his vision of the cosmos is rhetorically significant. Many modern readers jump to the dragon and beasts as the focal point of interest; but for John the key figures in this drama are not the "bad guys." God and the Lamb, not the beast, occupy center stage.

This is in itself an attack on Roman imperial ideology, which depicted the emperor (and the gods that give him his power) at the center of the conceptual universe. [Fig. 3.1.]

John opens his unveiling, his apocalypse, with a vision of perfect order, with all created beings in concentric spheres looking in toward the true center of the cosmos, worshiping God and the Lamb as they deserve. First a figurative door in the dome of the sky has to crack open before mortals can peer into that realm beyond visible realities (4:2). There God sits enthroned, surrounded first by four "living creatures" resembling the seraphim or other angelic attendants in earlier throne visions (4:6–8; compare Isa 6:2–3; Ezek 1:5–11). Seven spirits, best understood as the seven high-ranking archangels or angels of the Presence, stand next in attendance around the throne (4:5b). Twenty-four elders sitting upon their thrones (4:4) form a further circle around God's throne. Around these, in ever-widening circles, move angels in the ten thousands of ten thousands (5:11). All of these superhuman creatures are focused on the Enthroned One and the Lamb, offering continual worship and adoration. Finally, at the furthest reaches of this map, John places "every creature in heaven and on earth and under the earth and in the sea" (5:13 NRSV), united in directing praise and adoration toward the center of the cosmos, God and the Lamb: "Blessing and honor and glory and power forever and ever to the One seated upon the throne and to the Lamb!" (Rev 5:13). If there is a true "universal consent," it upholds not the reign of the emperors, but the reign of the God of Israel and this God's Messiah.

The hymns they sing remind John's audience of the grounds for such worship and thanksgiving.

> "You are worthy, our Lord and God, to receive glory and honor and power, for you created all things, and by your will they existed and were created." (Rev 4:11 NRSV)

The first hymn declares that God deserves public acknowledgment (glory), honor, and power *because* God has created all that is. The unstated premise here is the universally held conviction that benefactors (among whom God is supreme) merit a grateful response, typically including honor and service. The one Creator God is worthy of worship, and the benefaction of the gift of life itself requires a response of obedience, living that life in accordance with God's commandments, which includes the prohibition of worshiping any other would-be divinity.

The second hymn celebrates the unique authority that belongs by right to the Lamb:

> "You are worthy to take the scroll and to open its seals, for you were slaughtered and by your blood you ransomed for God saints from every tribe and language and people and nation; you have made them to be a kingdom and priests serving our God, and they will reign on earth. . . . Worthy is the Lamb that was slaughtered to receive power and wealth and wisdom and might and honor and glory and blessing!" (Rev 5:9–12 NRSV)

The authority to take this scroll from the hand of God and to open its seals, we soon find out, translates to the authority to set in motion the events that bring about the final judgment upon the earthly kingdoms and that usher in God's kingdom—to bring "the kingdoms of the world" under the complete authority of "the kingdom of our Lord and of his Messiah" (11:15 NRSV). This authority belongs to the Lamb "by right," because the Lamb redeemed a people for God to constitute that kingdom, giving up his own life on their behalf, fulfilling at last the promise of the creation of a priestly kingdom. In so doing, the Lamb exemplifies supreme beneficence, giving himself fully in the interest of the many rather than acting out of self-interest, rendering an important service to people in significant need (since "redeeming" or "ransoming" suggests a situation of significant distress). Therefore, the Lamb also merits gratitude in the highest degree.

Notice also how John has set the stage for the Lamb's coming forward. An angel issues a challenge:

> " 'Who is worthy to open the scroll and break its seals?' But no one in heaven or on earth or under the earth could open the scroll or look inside it. So I began to weep and weep, because no one was found worthy to open the scroll or to look inside it." (Rev 5:3–4)

No one can step into that silence, and for all his pretensions, the emperor, the alleged "savior" of the known world, is also unworthy of this ultimate honor. It is Jesus—the slaughtered Lamb (notably, slaughtered under Rome)—who has the greater worthiness, who has shown more worthily what it means to serve God's design for humanity and to act as a perfect bene-factor. In this picture of the cosmic order, where is there room to worship another?

It quickly becomes clear that this vision of the perfectly ordered cosmos is a vision of the way things *ought* to be, but not of the way things *are* in every corner of the cosmos. The Lamb has redeemed a people "out from every tribe and lan-guage and people and nation," but this leaves people in those tribes, language groups, peoples, and nations who are not part of that redeemed body, people who are out of line with the cosmic order in which "all creatures" acknowledge God and the Lamb with due honor and grateful obedience.

When, with John, we look away from the center back to-ward the earth again, we see who these deviant people are more clearly. There are some who are bucking against the "universal consensus" that acknowledges the reign of God and the Lamb. There are signs of significant pockets of resistance to, even re-bellion against, the divine order. There are people who, in the face of the proclamation about this One God and even in the face of experiencing this God's judgments, refuse "to repent of the works of their hands or give up worshiping demons and idols of gold and silver and bronze and stone and wood, which cannot see or hear or walk" (Rev 9:20 NRSV).

John pulls off quite a coup. The vast *majority* of people liv-ing around the Mediterranean basin worshiped multiple gods and goddesses, almost always incorporating idols as visible rep-resentations of their deities into their worship sites and rituals. This was evident, for example, in our brief tours of Ephesus and Pergamum. The cults of Rome and the emperors, in particular, invoked a mental picture for the worshipers in which Rome was the center of the universe, as the center of power in the Mediterranean. Jews and Christians were deviant minorities, turning away from such cultic centers to perform their own rites to their tribal God in the conceptual margins of the city.

In John's vision, however, the worshipers of idols are the deviant minority. The hosts of heaven, together with "every creature in heaven and on earth and below the earth," recognize the true center of the cosmos, and thus where to direct adoration properly, and the minority Christian groups are attuned to this order. Those who worship the Greco-Roman divinities are the ones looking in the wrong directions around a false center, aligned with "demons," the associates of Satan, the archenemy of God and of the cosmic order (see Rev 13:4). Writers like Paul and the author of Baruch, incidentally, also reflect the idea that the worship offered to idols was, in fact, given to demons (see Bar 4:6–7; 1 Cor 10:14–21).

The dramatic action of Revelation focuses on how the forces from the heavenly "center" break into and overrun the realities around the seven congregations. John narrates a future in which everything that is "out of order" is set *back* in order vis-à-vis the centrality of God and the Lamb and their just requirements, or else eliminated (by virtue of being deposited in the receptacle of the lake of fire) if it resists being brought back in line.

The wheels are set in motion by the opening of the seven seals of the scroll, leading to a pair of scenes in which human beings encounter God and the Lamb. The first scene is one of abject terror:

> The sun became black as funeral clothing, and the entire moon turned red as blood. The stars of the sky fell to the earth as a fig tree drops its fruit when shaken by a strong wind. The sky disappeared like a scroll being rolled up, and every mountain and island was moved from its place. Then the kings of the earth, the officials and the generals, the rich and the powerful, and everyone, slave and free, hid themselves in caves and in the rocks of the mountains. They called to the mountains and the rocks, "Fall on us and hide us from the face of the one seated on the throne and from the Lamb's wrath! The great day of their wrath has come, and who is able to stand?" (Rev 6:12–17 CEB)

The hearers are themselves implicitly included in this response, for it is not only the kings and potentates, but also "*every* slave and free person" who trembles before God and the Lamb (6:15). This sounds a strange counterpoint to Rev 5:13, where "every creature" shouts in worship rather than in fear: John's presentation of universal, contradictory visions highlights the alternatives he sets before his congregations. The hearers are driven to "see" themselves in both scenes, to experience the accompanying feelings, and thus to resolve themselves to remain consistently centered on God and the Lamb in all their doings.

The scene of panic ends with the rhetorical question borrowed from the older prophetic text, Malachi: "Who shall stand when he appears?!" (Mal 3:2). The answer is found in the following scene of the 144,000 and the uncountable number who are seen *standing* (7:9) before God's throne:

> After this I looked, and there was a great crowd that no one could number. They were from every nation, tribe, people, and language. They were standing before the throne and before the Lamb. They wore white robes and held palm branches in their hands. . . . "This is the reason they are before God's throne. They worship him day and night in his temple, and the one seated on the throne will shelter them. They won't hunger or thirst anymore. No sun or scorching heat will beat down on them, because the Lamb who is in the midst of the throne will shepherd them. He will lead them to the springs of life-giving water, and God will wipe away every tear from their eyes." (Rev 7:9, 15–17 CEB)

Before the terror of the coming of God and the Lamb on the day of their wrath, a terror that is so severe that it simply cannot be *faced* (6:16–17), there is only one remedy, one path to relief and safety—to remain a faithful witness to God and to the Lamb, and to keep oneself unentangled from the sins of the Roman imperial system, no matter what temporary disadvantages or deprivations that entails.

John's opening visions invite rather direct appropriation among churches in every age, since the scenes into which the readers and hearers project themselves belong, in John's own worldview and the worldview fostered by Nicene Christianity, to the eternal, cosmic realm or to the realm of the eschatological future. The vision of cosmic worship is an eternal reality, though the opening of the scroll itself marks the incursion of those heavenly realities into the sphere of history. The visions of those standing victorious before the throne of God or cowering in fear before God's burning anger on the "Day of Wrath" belong to the post-historical future. As such, these scenes beckon us still to imagine ourselves within them and to examine ourselves and our discipleship from the perspective of these scenes.

The vision of all creation centered in worship and obedient waiting upon God and God's Messiah invites us first of all into the experience of God's throne as the pivotal center of our lives, prompting us to make this the focal point of our corporate worship and our personal prayer and meditation. John calls us to center ourselves, and to remain centered, *here*. This centering for John does not belong to the fleeting moments of structured times of worship, however. It is the business of God's creatures "day and night without rest" (4:8), which for human beings must mean bringing every facet of life into orbit around the enthroned God, centered on God, on God's prompting, on God's service. In John's vision of the cosmos, there is no room for gathering around God's throne at one time as one's cosmic center and at another time in the fellowship of idols and their worshipers.

There are prophets and teachers among the seven churches who are, in fact, promoting the opposite, domesticating the demands of a unique, Creator God to the practical needs of functioning in, and profiting from, the domination systems of the real world. John challenges us to examine whether we stand appropriately focused on God on Sunday mornings but spend most of our time (and, truth be told, some of Sunday morning as well) turning away to move into orbit around other more local centers—our national centers, our commercial centers, the centers of our own selves—serving agendas other than God's. As I myself consider how we tend to invoke God and involve God in the religious settings of which I am a part, I find John's vision of a God-centered cosmos raising even more disturbing questions about whether or not we are guilty of treating God as if he orbited around us, expecting God to show up to do our bidding, warming our hearts here, healing us there, taking care of this concern or problem over here. John would have disciples in every age understand—and live like they understand—that they exist to do *God's* bidding, because God created all things for the doing of God's will and pleasure (4:11).

Roman imperialism: The untold story

When John takes us to look even closer into the activity of the world in rebellion against God, we see a movement afoot to steal away the worship due the One God and to draw as many people as possible into a lie that leads them away from the true center. John thoroughly dismantles the dominant culture's story. From the point of view of the throne of the One God and his Christ, Roman power, the emperor, and the worship offered to both everywhere look quite different. Indeed, by reminding his churches of the awe and gratitude due the Creator God and the Redeemer Lamb, the genuine Savior and Son of the Divine (Rev 4–5), John laid the groundwork for evoking indignation against the pretensions of promoters of the cult of Rome and the *Augusti* in these later visions.

First, in Revelation 12–13, John completely rewrites the ideology of the head of empire. John takes the four beasts of Daniel 7, representing in sequence the kingdoms of Bablyon, Persia, Greece, and Alexander's successors, and combines them into a single, unholy hybrid to represent Roman rule and Rome's heads of state. Roman imperialism brings together all that the previous empires had contained, in terms of geography, power, and bestial corruption. The unnatural, animal imagery hides the humanness of the emperor and negates any legitimate claims he might have to the gratitude or loyalty of the audiences. The *Augusti* appear as a monstrous aberration, prodigious in the worst sense. Like Daniel before him in regard to earlier empires, John invites his audience to regard the character and rule of Rome's emperors as something out of all harmony with the divine and natural orders.

The "beast's" origins are not what the public story claims. The rule of the *Augusti* does not spring from some benign Providence seeking to order human life well, but from the rebellion of Satan, the source of all chaos and disorder, against God. After Satan is defeated in the heavenly realm, Satan invests his power in this beast as part of his last-ditch attempt to deceive people and lead them astray from God's truth, knowing "that his time is short" (Rev 12:11): "It stood upon the shore of the sea. And I saw a beast coming up out of the sea.

. . . The dragon gave it his power, throne, and great authority" (Rev 12:18–13:2). Where the Christians' neighbors would accept that Zeus gave the emperors their authority, John draws upon the conviction that the worship given to idols is given, in actuality, to demonic forces, with Zeus representing the chief of those forces. Therefore, Satan ultimately stands behind Roman power.

The emperors themselves are not pious figures or mediators of divine favor, as the public image of them declares. Rather, they are founts of blasphemy against God (Rev 13:1, 5, 6). The emperor's divine titles (typically including "son of a god," *divi filius*) are illegitimate, the "names of blasphemy" that offend the Most High. Flattering courtiers in Rome and local authorities in Asia Minor addressed their emperors as "lord and God": what was for most of Asia Minor a matter of gratitude and welcome security was, for John, an insult to the one Lord and one God in the highest degree. Indeed, many of the titles ascribed to God and the Lamb throughout Revelation are stolen back by John from the emperor for the True God and for Christ throughout Revelation. The title "Lord of lords," for example, was ascribed to the emperor; the acclamations of God and Christ as "worthy" (4:11; 5:9) echo the sorts of acclamations with which citizens greeted their emperor. And Zeus or Jupiter, the highest god whose power stood behind the emperor, was lauded with the formula "Zeus was, Zeus is, Zeus will be, O great Zeus!," now taken over by John and transformed for the One God, "who was, and is, and is coming." The shift (from "will be" to "is coming") is significant: *this* God is on the way to encounter his creation and intervene once more in human affairs.

John challenges the public story that it was in response to Augustus's beneficence and investment of himself in the public good that he received "universal consent" to rule. In John's presentation, "the whole earth marveled at the beast . . . and worshiped the beast, saying, 'Who is like the beast, and who can make war against it?'" (Rev 13:3–4). The second part of this rationale for worship is telling: whereas the Lamb's authority is acknowledged by universal consent on the more noble and praiseworthy basis of his other-centered sacrifice, the emperors received and maintain it on the basis of military might and the use of violence as the mechanism for unifying multiple peoples, languages, nations, and tribes into "empire."

The beast and Satan—God's enemies and rivals of the Lamb for sway over humankind—enjoy what they do not deserve, namely, worship. John uses parody to highlight the counterfeit nature of the worship going on all around the churches. The beast worshipers ask, "Who is like the beast?" (13:4), a rhetorical question implying that there is no one equal to this great and powerful being. Throughout the Scriptures, however, John's audience would have encountered this same rhetorical question, but asked in regard to the One God:

> "Who is like you among the gods, Lord?
> Who is like you, glorified among the holy ones?" (Exod 15:11)

> "Lord, who is like you?" (Ps 35:10 NRSV)

> "O God, who is like you?" (Ps 71:19 NRSV)

The inhabitants of the earth acclaim the beast using a phrase, then, stolen from the worship of God, even as the worship offered to the beast and the dragon itself is worship stolen from the God to whom it is uniquely due as Creator of all that is, sharpening the impropriety and injustice of this cult of the beast.

In a parody of Christ's legitimate bringing together of a people for God from every "tribe and language and people and nation" (Rev 5:9), the beast from the sea seeks to exercise rule over the members of every "tribe and people and language and nation" (Rev 13:7), and indeed the imperial cult was a powerful tool for unifying the many different people groups now brought under the aegis of Rome. A second, local beast organizes religious cult for the first beast, making the worship of the beast a requirement for continued economic and physical well-being:

> I saw another beast coming up from the earth. . . . It also makes the earth and those who live in it worship the first beast, whose fatal wound was healed. . . . It told those who live on earth to make an image for the beast who had been wounded by the sword and yet came to life again. . . . It forces everyone—the

small and great, the rich and poor, the free and slaves—to have a mark put on their right hand or on their forehead. It will not allow anyone to make a purchase or sell anything unless the person has the mark with the beast's name or the number of its name. (Rev 13:11, 12, 14, 16, 17 CEB)

Again, this is a reversal of the majority view of the imperial cult, understood as a pious response of gratitude to a great benefactor, something freely, even enthusiastically, and rightly offered to the one seated upon the throne in Rome. John sees it as an imposition from those in power, not a voluntary cult, giving poignant expression to the pressures Christians felt and would soon feel all the more.

Once again, the ultimate recipient of such cult is not a benign deity, but the dragon, the Enemy of God, whose worship is linked to that of the beast (Rev 13:4), even as the cults of the traditional gods were frequently linked to the imperial cult: "All the earth marveled after the beast and they worshiped the *dragon*, because he gave authority to the beast, and they worshiped the beast" (13:3b–4a). In John's understanding, it is not the Christians who act seditiously by withdrawing from participation in the cults of Rome and the Roman gods, but the supporters of Rome who rebel against the rule of the Most High God and his Anointed. The only kind of person who could participate in such cults is a person whose name "hadn't been written—from the time the earth was made—in the scroll of life of the lamb who was slain" (13:8).

John uses Nero as a kind of symbol to characterize the Principate. While the "mortal wound" affects the beast as a whole and not merely one of its heads (13:3, 12, 14), the swordblow to one of its heads cannot help but recall Nero's suicide. The detail that a future "head" will come, in fact, from one of those that have fallen, is perhaps the clearest echo of the popular legend of "Nero come back from the dead" in the book (17:11). But Nero is not merely one aberrant head among others: he gives the beast its character. When John comes to the topic of the beast's number, he says: "This calls for wisdom. Let the one who understands calculate the beast's number, for it's a human being's number. Its number is six hundred sixty-six"

(Rev 13:18). Latin, Greek, and Hebrew all use letters to represent not only sounds, but also numerals. When John identifies the "number of the beast's name" as 666, he is inviting his audience to figure out whose name has letters that, taken as their numerical equivalents, add up to 666. In my opinion, the best solution remains Nero Caesar, as written and added up in Hebrew. In Hebrew, $n = 50$, $r = 200$, $w = 6$, $q = 100$, and $s = 60$. Thus *nrwn qsr* ("Nero Caesar") adds up to 666. John invites the hearers thus to see in Nero—and in Nero's distinctive persecution of Roman Christians and their leaders—the true character of the Principate, bare, exposed in all its ugliness and its opposition to the reign of Christ.

In this subversive portrait, John also questions the public claims made about a *pax Augusta* or *pax Romana*—a "peace" secured and preserved by Augustus and his successors, a benefit of unity under Roman rule. A prominent element of Roman imperial ideology was the claim that the rise of the Principate had brought "peace" to the *orbis terrarum*. John exposes *Pax Romana* and *Pax Augusta* to be bald-faced lies. He does not allow his hearers to ignore the fact that a great deal of violence has gone into creating and sustaining empire, for example, in the brutal suppression of the Jewish Revolt. How is it truly a matter of "peace" if you use overwhelming force to subdue a country that never wished to be a part of your empire in the first place?

The *Pax Romana* is also, in fact, a time of "making war with the saints" (13:7), "making war" with the witnesses of Jesus, conquering and killing them (11:7). With the opening of the fifth seal, John identifies a pressing cause for the judgments that are coming:

> I saw under the altar those who had been slaughtered on account of the word of God and the witness they had given. They cried out with a loud voice, "Holy and true Master, how long will you wait before you pass judgment? How long before you require justice for our blood, which was shed by those who live on earth?" Each of them was given a white robe, and they were told to rest a little longer, until their fellow servants and brothers and sisters—who were about to be killed as they were—were finished. (Rev 6:9–11 CEB)

The souls of Christian martyrs cry out for justice; later, two angels will praise the justice of God for punishing "Babylon" and its allies for violently snuffing out the lives of saints and prophets (16:5–7; 18:24). While it is unlikely that Revelation was written during a period of open persecution, the memory of the Christian holocausts in Rome, as well as more local and individual actions against Christians such as Antipas (2:13), has not dissipated in John's mind. Roman rule is the rule of violence, spilling not only the blood of holy ones and the witnesses of Jesus (17:6), but of "all those who had been slain upon the earth" (18:23b–24). It is a time in which those destined for slaughter by the sword and for captivity meet their destiny (13:10). Moreover, the guardians of the "Roman peace" are the pawns of Satan, deployed as part of a last ditch effort within a cosmic revolt that continues to play itself out as Revelation nears its climax. This portrait of a world, indeed a cosmos, at war evokes an attitude of resistance against the forces that John places in the enemy's camp, steering the audience away from cooperation and compromise.

And what of *Roma Aeterna*, "Eternal Rome," the beneficent goddess whose worship was everywhere yoked to the cult of the emperor? John creates one of the most memorable—and negative—pictures of Rome in extant literature. He tells a very different story about the mission and the destiny of *Roma Aeterna* from the one heard in Virgil's *Aeneid* or Plutarch's *On the Fortune of Rome*.

First, John presents the goddess *Roma* in very different dress. No longer wearing the modest toga of the goddess worshiped in the temple of Rome and the *Augusti*, nor even the austere military garb in which she appears on the reverse of the famous *Dea Roma* coin [Fig. 3.2, see p. 63.], here she's dressed in her evening wear, sporting the lingerie of a self-employed courtesan and plying her trade with the utmost success. [Fig. 3.3, see p. 63.] Her impact on the civilized world is entirely negative. Her résumé includes plundering the wealth of the provinces to satisfy her taste for luxury, murdering countless holy ones, witnesses to Jesus, and others who have dissented against or hindered her practices, and seducing the leaders of the inhabited world into forming unholy alliances to promote

Fig. 1.3a. A cult statue of Diana/
Artemis discovered at Ephesus.
The image in the great Temple of
Artemis closely resembled this smaller
version (Photo: David deSilva).

Fig. 1.3b. Silver cistophorus
(tetradrachm) of Claudius (emperor,
41–54 C.E.), the reverse showing
the cult statue of Diana (Artemis)
standing in her celebrated Temple
in Ephesus, and silver cistophorus
of Hadrian (emperor, 117–138
C.E.) with the cult statue of
Diana (Artemis) in sharper detail
on the reverse, bearing witness
to the persistence of this image's
importance in the province of Asia.
Courtesy of Classical Numismatic
Group, Inc. (www.CNGcoins.com).

Fig. 1.4. The Acropolis of Pergamum. The white, columned
ruins of the Temple of Trajan dominate the upper left. The site
of the monumental Altar of Zeus is marked by the large trees in
the upper center. A Temple of Athena originally stood above the
amphitheatre. The ruins of the Temple of Dionysus are visible halfway
down the hill from Trajan's Temple (Photo: David deSilva).

Fig. 1.5. The site of the Altar of Zeus, overlooking Pergamum/Bergama. The prominent location of this altar on the brow of the acropolis recommends it as the local monument referred to as "Satan's throne" in the oracle to the Christians in Pergamum (Photo: David deSilva).

Fig. 1.6. The monumental Altar of Zeus at the Pergamon Museum, Berlin. The carved reliefs surrounding the structure depict scenes from the mythic battle of the Olympian gods against the giants. Courtesy of Wikipedia Commons (Photo: Jan Mehlich).

Fig. 1.7. Temple of Dionysus, Pergamum. This temple is a short walk from the base of the great ampitheater carved into the hill of the acropolis. There is a historic connection between the performance of dramas (particularly tragedies) and festivals honoring Dionysus (Photo: David deSilva).

Fig. 1.8. Temple of Demeter, Pergamum (Photo: David deSilva).

Fig. 1.9. Cult scene, Temple of Demeter. A small part of a bas relief decorating the altar of the Temple of Demeter on the Pergamum acropolis. A priestess stands between the sacrificial animal and the sacred fire on the altar (Photo: David deSilva).

Fig. 1.12. Temple of Julius Caesar and *Roma*, Ephesus.
This temple sat adjacent to the Prytaneion, the "city
hall" of Ephesus (Photo: David deSilva).

Fig. 1.13. The Plateau of the Temple of Domitian (the Flavian Temple) in Ephesus. The Flavian Temple originally stood over the flat, grassy space above the arches that formed part of its foundation. From this place, it dominated the civic spaces of Ephesus (Photo: David deSilva).

Fig. 1.15. Original Harbor of Ephesus. The harbor of ancient
Ephesus is now little more than a swamp because of centuries of
silting. In ancient times, this harbor gave Ephesus direct access
to the Aegean Sea and made it a major center for trade and
commerce in the Mediterranean (Photo: David deSilva).

Fig. 2.2. Sesterce of Nero (emperor, 54–68 C.E.). The reverse features the goddess Roma seated, holding a representation of victory (*Nikē*) in her right hand. Courtesy of Classical Numismatic Group, Inc. (www.CNGcoins.com).

Fig. 2.3a. Denarius of Trajan (emperor, 98–117 C.E.). The reverse shows the personification of "the Providence of the *Augusti*," the divine principle that gives stability (signified by the pillar on which Providence rests) to the whole world (the globe at her feet). Courtesy of Classical Numismatic Group, Inc. (www.CNGcoins.com).

Fig. 2.3b. Bronze as (1/16 of a denarius) of Nero (emperor, 54–69 C.E.). The "Altar of Peace" erected by Augustus adorns the reverse. Courtesy of Classical Numismatic Group, Inc. (www.CNGcoins.com).

Fig. 2.4. Part of the marble lintel that originally stood atop the Fountain of Trajan in Ephesus. The inscription reads, "[*Hē N*]*eōkoros Ephesiōn Polis*," "The Temple-Warden City of the Ephesians" (Photo: David deSilva).

Fig. 2.5. Detail of an inscription in the gymnasium in Pergamum, honoring the director of the facility. The Pergamenes describe themselves here as "The First-to-be-Awarded the Temple Wardenship" of the imperial cult in the province of Asia (Photo: David deSilva).

Fig. 2.6a. Temple of Trajan (emperor, 98–117 C.E.), Pergamum.
After its construction, this temple dominated the acropolis, including
the Altar of Zeus, bearing witness to the ongoing importance of
imperial cult in the early second century (Photo: David deSilva).

Figs. 2.6b and 2.6b inset. An inscription from the Temple of
Trajan attests to the award of a second neokorate to Pergamum.
The words "*Dis Neōkoros*," "twice named Temple Warden,"
are clearly visible in the inset (Photos: David deSilva).

Fig. 2.7. An inscription from the Asklepion outside of Pergamum bears witness to the city's continued claim to preeminence in the province based on its devotion to the imperial cult after Ephesus was awarded its second Neocorate. Pergamum remained "first to be named 'twice Temple Warden'" (Photo: David deSilva).

Fig. 2.8. Denarius of Tiberius, with Peace (thought also to represent Livia, Tiberius's mother) seated on the reverse. The legend on the obverse is shorthand for "Tiberius Caesar Augustus, Son of the Deified Augustus," and the legend on the reverse for "Highest Priest." Courtesy of Classical Numismatic Group, Inc. (www.CNGcoins.com).

Fig. 3.3. *Prostituta da Babilônia* ("The Whore of Babylon") by Fernando Real. Courtesy of Folhapress, Brazil. [Fig. 3.2: Inset. By way of contrast note again (see Fig. 2.10.) the Sesterce of Vespasian, reverse, featuring the goddess *Roma* reclining against Rome's seven hills. Courtesy of Numismatica Ars Classica NAC AG (auction 54, lot 361).]

Fig. 3.4. Sesterce of Vespasian. Reverse legend reads *Iudea Capta*, "Judea Taken." A Jewish male captive stands beside a palm tree with his hands bound behind him; a Jewess (perhaps representing the province itself) sits on the ground and mourns. The minting commemorates Vespasian and Titus's suppression of the Jewish Revolt of 66–70 C.E. Courtesy of the Classical Numismatic Group, Inc. (www.CNGcoins.com).

Fig. 4.1. Denarius of Titus (emperor, 79–81 C.E.). The reverse features the façade of the Temple of Jupiter on the Capitoline Hill in Rome. The coin celebrates the renovation of this historic worship site. Courtesy of the Classical Numismatic Group, Inc. (www.CNGcoins.com).

Fig. 4.2. A Tyrian shekel, minted 107 B.C.E. This was the currency in which the temple tax had historically been paid, the tax that was diverted after 70 C.E. to subvent the costs of the restoration and operation of the Temple of Jupiter in Rome. Courtesy of Robert Deutsch, Archaeological Center, Jaffa (auction 48, lot 17; www.archaeological-center.com).

their collective self-indulgent practices. There is nothing here of *Roma* as the chosen vessel by means of which Providence renews a Golden Age; rather, her cup is full of abominations and the unclean residue of Rome's fornication.

John helps his audiences to look at Rome and Roman imperialism especially through the lens of the Hebrew prophets, who had long ago spoken against the self-serving practices of empires as contrary to God's good will for human beings in every nation. In particular, he accuses Rome of (1) violence against dissenters, especially against Jews and Christians; (2) economic exploitation, nurturing a system that caters to the luxury of the powerful at the expense of the many; and (3) idolatrous presumption in its claims on its own behalf. John develops each of these in such a way as to arouse indignation against Roman imperialism, supporting his call to Christians to keep themselves free from supporting or participating in such an unjust system of domination.

John gives attention throughout Revelation to Rome's violence, refusing to allow the public rhetoric of "peace" or "stability" to mask the violence with which that "peace" has been forged and continues to be maintained. The "mother of whores" is "drunk with the blood of the saints and the blood of the witnesses to Jesus" (Rev 17:6). She is responsible for "the blood of prophets and of saints, and of all who have been slaughtered on earth" (Rev 18:24 NRSV), and this very fact necessitates divine vengeance upon Rome, just as it did upon historic Babylon (Rev 18:20; cf. 6:9–11; 16:5–7).

Empire is forged out of conquest. A few territories came under Roman control peaceably as did, notably, Asia Minor. More, however, were "taken" by military force rather than "received." Coins bearing the inscription *Asia Recepta* commemorate Asia's peaceful submission to Roman rule. This stands in stark contrast to coins celebrating the "taking" of Egypt and Armenia, or the [re-]taking of Judea (*Aegypto Capta*, a minting featured under Octavian in 28 B.C.E.; *Armenia Capta*, another minting under Augustus; *Iudea Capta*, from multiple mintings commemorating the suppression of the First Jewish Revolt [Fig. 3.4, see p. 64.]). Such conquests came with heavy casualties. John's scenes of blood filling valleys and endless flocks of carrion birds gathering to feast upon the flesh of kings and soldiers are not products of apocalyptic imagination. They were available to be seen throughout John's lifetime (for example, in the Jewish Revolt or the suppression of smaller revolts throughout the East). Most criminals deemed seditious died by one of the most economical and cruel forms of punishment ever devised—economical because it required only some reusable wood and nails, but lasting for days as a deterrent to others who might disturb the Roman peace. The bloodbath in Rome under Nero, especially targeting Christians, showed the fragility of the protection afforded by law, long remaining a traumatic blot on the memory of Roman rule among conscientious Christians. Even a man as highly placed in the empire as the Roman historian Tacitus could see what Rome looked like "from the outside." Imagining how a German chieftain would have commented on the advancing Roman army, he writes: "to violence, rapine, and plunder they give the name, 'government'; they make a desert, and call it 'peace'" (*Agr.* 30).

John criticizes the Roman imperial economy as a system of self-interest structured chiefly to benefit Rome. The elites and inhabitants of Rome consumed disproportionate wealth and goods in great measure to indulge excessive desires and cravings (what John calls "luxury" in Rev 18:3, 7), while the poor in Rome's provinces were often short even on the necessities of life. The gaudiness of the great prostitute, draped in luxurious clothing ("purple and scarlet"), richly adorned ("gold and precious stones and pearls"), and sporting luxury goods (not just a cup, but a "golden cup"; Rev 17:4) highlights the visceral commitment to excess and self-indulgence that John saw in the Roman economy. He captures it again in his focus on the extensive cargoes flowing from the ports throughout the known world, taking both staples (like grain and oil) and luxury items away from the provinces, where they are produced, to satiate a single city's cravings (18:12–13). We should remember that part of what Rome enjoyed came to her by way of trade, but another large part came by way of tribute—the enormous sums of money that each province collected and sent to Rome for the support of Rome's army, Rome's empire-wide building and military operations, and Rome's lifestyle.

The Roman economy included the provision of free grain and oil for the city of Rome's 200,000 families on the "dole"—a perk of living in the capital of the empire. As John watches the cargoes of "wine and oil and fine flour and grain" streaming toward Rome (Rev 18:13), he watches the prices of staples like barley and wheat rise in the provinces where the grains are grown. Rome purchased these grains inexpensively from the provinces in fixed minimum quantities and at fixed prices. This meant that the residents of the provinces often had to pay inflated prices for the insufficient amounts of grain that were left, and in times of shortage went without. The situation was made worse as local landowners used more and more of their land to produce crops that brought in a better financial yield per arable acre. Market demands made the production of oil and wine far more attractive, often leading to scarcity in the essentials of wheat and barley in the provinces. Revelation 6:5–6 reflects a situation in which the prices of staples are grossly inflated, while production of oil and wine proceeds unabated.

> When [the Lamb] opened the third seal, I heard the third living creature say, "Come!" So I looked, and there was a black horse. Its rider held a balance for weighing in his hand. I heard what sounded like a voice from among the four living creatures. It said, "A quart of wheat for a denarion, and three quarts of barley for a denarion, but don't damage the olive oil and the wine." (Rev 6:5–6 CEB)

John calls attention to the parasitic side of the Roman imperial economy, countering any feelings of gratitude toward Rome by drawing attention to the pervasive self-interest that underlies Roman rule. *Roma* is an anti-benefactor, whose influence and interventions ultimately seek to secure self-serving ends. John includes no notice of anything Rome has done purely on behalf of her subjects. The emphasis on luxury, intemperance, and conspicuous consumption also nurtures indignation, as Rome is seen to consume more of the world's goods than any one city, enjoying more than is due—and this often to the detriment of the provinces under her far-from-beneficent rule. If Rome brings prosperity, she does so only to the merchants and shipmasters and others who profit (or profiteer) as they direct the world's wealth and resources to her ravenous maw.

The Roman economy was, furthermore, built and maintained upon the backs of slaves, humans sufficiently dehumanized to be spoken of as simply "bodies" or, in Aristotle's infamous phrase, "living tools." Approximately one quarter of the population of the empire was enslaved. While slaves lived under conditions that ran the gamut from desperate to luxurious, they shared this basic definition and the vulnerability it implied for their identity and security as persons. John draws attention to this facet of the Roman economy—indeed, its bedrock—by listing "bodies, that is, human lives" in the inventory of the cargo that streams toward Rome from every quadrant of the *orbis terrarum*. In his list of twenty-eight items in Rev 18:12–13, John has given "bodies" the climactic position by placing it last and heightened emphasis by providing this brief gloss.

The Roman economy also undermined resistance to Roman domination among non-Roman elites by cultivating a desire in them for what Rome had and could provide for her willing partners. John may have this in mind as he speaks of the great whore seducing the inhabitants and the kings of the earth. The Roman historian Tacitus, writing perhaps only a decade after John, attested to the fact that growing fond of and accustomed to the luxury goods and entertainments introduced with the Roman presence undermined resistance to Roman rule. As he writes his histories, he imagines a general among the north German tribes exhorting his people: "Away with those pleasures which give the Romans more power over their subjects than their arms bestow!" (*Hist.* 4.64.3). The Romans might strategically introduce luxury items and offer the "privilege" of Greek and Roman education for the children of local elites in places where there was resistance in order to achieve by such seduction what force could not effect as efficiently.

The wealth to be enjoyed by participating in the larger global economy was, as far as John was concerned, a dangerous lure toward sharing in the violence and political injustice that undergirded such an economy, as well as sharing in the economic injustice that allowed the resources and produce of the provinces to be siphoned off to satisfy the immoderate cravings of Rome's inhabitants and worldwide elite. John understood long before the modern era that a person cannot share in the profits of domination without also sharing in responsibility for its crimes: "Come out of her, my people, so that you don't take part in her sins and don't receive any of her plagues" (Rev 18:4 CEB).

And, of course, Rome claimed honor (Rev 18:7) beyond what was rightly hers to claim, and the cult of the goddess *Roma* would have been an especially egregious offense in John's eyes. Related to this charge is the presumption inherent in the public discourse about Rome as the "Eternal City," *Roma Aeterna*, claiming for Rome what has never belonged to any kingdom or empire before her: "In her heart she says, 'I sit like a queen! I'm not a widow. I'll never see grief.' This is why her plagues will come in a single day—deadly disease, grief, and hunger. She will be consumed by fire because the Lord God who judges her is powerful" (Rev 18:7–8 CEB). Such arrogance signals Rome's refusal to apply the lessons of history to a more humble and humane rule.

John knows a God who allots to all kingdoms their times and seasons, and history has never known a kingdom that has failed to fall from its height into obscurity and subjugation to other kingdoms. God intervenes to bring low those rulers or empires that forget and affront God's sovereign oversight. Rome's claims about its divinity and destiny are textbook examples of the arrogant presumption of imperialist thinking. John exposes these pretensions in his vision of Rome's demise, which will reveal the emptiness of Rome's claims in favor of the persistent truth that all human domination systems run their course. Every seat of empire, no matter how prosperous at its peak, will one day sit as a ruin, and Rome will be no different (Rev 18:2). The "Eternal City" stands under God's imminent judgment, sentenced already to destruction for her crimes against "apostles, saints, and prophets," and will surely go up in smoke and be laid desolate rather than live up to its name. The scene of the great prostitute stripped, naked, devoured by her allies, and burned up (17:16–17) is John's final answer to Rome's self-glorifying propaganda.

Exerting control and maintaining peace through violent suppression of dissent; promoting an economy arranged for the great benefit of the few; the prominent use of religious language and ritual to legitimate these arrangements—this is both the genius of Rome and the heap of her sins for which John excoriates her. To enter into partnership with Rome is to fall victim to its deceit (Rev 18:23), which intoxicates the ignorant (Rev 17:2), and thus to be united with her in her sins and their punishment at the hands of the just and judging God.

We know how John's story ends. Babylon is judged at last and left a wasteland. God's Messiah returns to execute judgment upon all the forces hostile to God's rule. At last, a truly new society is founded—the New Jerusalem—which exists for the healing of the nations rather than for the conquest and exploitation of the same. All claims made on behalf of traditional Greco-Roman religion and on behalf of Roman imperialism are swept aside—or, better, exposed in the light of Scripture and in the light of the God that Scripture proclaims.

Applying John's lenses to our landscape

How would we apply John's critique of Roman imperialism and call for faithful response in the midst of the same to a modern context, if we resist the approach that seeks to name some person, country, or group "the beast" and some modern entity "the Whore of Babylon"? I would suggest that John would have us subject our own social, economic, and political systems, and our involvement in the same (both as disciples and as collective Christian bodies), to the same scrutiny that John subjected his own and that of his congregations, and to do this on the same basis. That basis would be the scriptural revelation of God's priorities and agenda for human community and God's commendation or censure of the practices that impede those priorities and that agenda. Revelation, therefore, suggests a model for ongoing engagement, examination, critique, and discernment of responses that embody faithful witness to God's purposes and even contribute to the creation of experiences, however fleeting, of the wholeness and justice that is central to God's purposes for humanity.

Thus John's precedent in Revelation summons us to ask: How do our country's economic practices, political entanglements, and ideologies look when measured up against the Israelite prophets, Jesus' teachings and example, and John's critique of his own imperial context? What values have we—as individual disciples and as groups of disciples (e.g., "churches")—internalized, and in what directions are we pulled, that run counter to the call of God to holiness and justice, to allegiance to the global family of faith, to setting the kingdom of God first? This calls for careful study both of the Scriptures, the frame of reference from which the examination takes place, and the real-life practices of our context and their effects on human beings within and outside our systems.

In this process, it is of the utmost importance that we listen to voices "from outside" if we are ever going to get some perspective on the systems of which we are a part and on the values and ways of doing things that we never think to question. John, himself in all probability an outsider to Roman Asia Minor, was able to bring a perspective to the situation of Christians in Roman Asia Minor that they themselves were not able to arrive at on their own. In my seminary classroom, my American students and I frequently benefit from listening to international students as they share their perspectives on the United States and on the church in the United States. They are often able to pinpoint inconsistencies between our practice and the scriptural vision that we overlook because of our primary socialization into our *country's* values and practice. We benefit in the classroom even more regularly from conversations between persons from very different social locations within the American context where, again, people from the inner city are able to help people in rural contexts see the realities more clearly than the images of the same portrayed in the media (and often in personal prejudices), where people from near-invisible minorities like indigenous Americans can bear witness to experiences of conquest and marginalization that call our public discourse about America into stark question. Christians in church settings often have to work a lot harder to gain this perspective, since congregations are often among the most homogeneous groups in our context.

And, of course, Scripture speaks a perennial "voice from outside," if we attend to it on its own terms. Again because of our immersion, often from birth, in the assumptions, values, goals, and practices of our own society and its systems, we have a tendency to domesticate the voice of Scripture so that Scripture can live in the house that we have built in our society, rather than invite Scripture to tell us how to rebuild the house from new foundations. One strategy for pushing past this is to be particularly attentive to the places where Jesus, Paul, James, or John rubs us the wrong way. Where do we say, in response to something we're reading in the New Testament, "No, he can't *possibly* mean *that*"? Where do we jump to find some consideration that will blunt the force of the challenge or demand the text poses, so that we can move on without letting that word change the way we think, live, or relate to others? Where do we find ourselves making excuses for our country ("Nations *have* to do that kind of thing") or for ourselves ("We've got to be practical as well, and not get carried away with this religion stuff")?

In some instances, the discomfort in the encounter comes from our awareness, two thousand years later, that not even the authors of Scripture completely escaped the assumptions, values, and practices of their own social world (such as their assumptions about slavery and gender roles), and so our hearing and following of their voices must be tempered accordingly. In many instances, however, I would expect such instances of discomfort to draw our attention to the ways in which *we* have drunk deep from Babylon's cup and are tempted to remain in our stupor. In such encounters, we need to allow the words of Jesus, Paul, John, and the rest strike us with full force, so as to sober us up and get us ready to stand before God at his coming with confidence, rather than in terror. John's model further challenges us to look at our world *consistently* against the witness of Scripture and the Spirit to what God values and what God desires for human community: we can't shift gears between a religious mode and a "practical" mode.

It might be of some benefit to look more closely at one particular example. Given John's interest in economic values and practices, among many other interests, I will take "consumerism" for this example. According to sociologist Barry Harvey,

> Christians in North America constitute, for the most part, a population that is not clearly distinguished from non-Christian North Americans in the modern world, assuming along with virtually everyone else that their purpose in life is to pursue their own interests in every sphere allotted to them by the institutions of our commercial republic. A majority of those who continue to call themselves Christian "retain a vague notion of religious identity but their lives are distinctively secular, with the experience of God in worship and prayer not figuring very prominently in all that they do. Increasingly these nominal Christian . . . Americans embrace the heady hedonism and narcissism of popular culture and do not see that this contradicts biblical faith" (Guroian 1994:89). Firmly ensconced in the well-worked tracks of the City, they regard religion almost exclusively as a private and inward matter, quite often as a form of therapy designed to make their lives more fulfilling. They see little or nothing wrong in regarding the church as simply another vendor of goods and services.[1]

Harvey observes that many American Christians live (and even think) in a way that agrees with the dominant culture's relegation of religion to the private, internal sphere, viewing religion as a commodity of self-help and self-actualization. Their approach to religion and to religious communities agrees with the "commodification" of religion and religious involvement as practices and experiences to be evaluated on the basis of how well they enhance one's sense of gratification and fulfillment. The testimonies that "I got a lot out of that service" and the complaint that "I don't get much out of going to that service" equally demonstrate the elevation of the "values" of consumerism and gratification as the uniting principles that join Christians in solidarity with their non-Christian, fellow Americans, who could evaluate their commitments and involvements in much the same way.

To the extent that this evaluation rings true, Christians are failing both to experience and to bear witness to the alternative orientation to the world (*and* to the problem of self) that

---

[1] Barry A. Harvey, *Another City: An Ecclesiological Primer for a Post-Christian World* (Harrisburg, PA: Trinity Press International, 1999), 3.

Jesus models and promotes when he empties himself, gives his life for the life of the world, and calls followers to deny themselves and find fullness in giving themselves away. One way to speak about the problem of "self" would be to speak about the problem of emptiness, the lack of fulfillment and fullness with which people wrestle. The legacy of modernity is "a self without substance, frantically searching for something, anything, to fill it up."[2] The self has become empty

> in part because of the loss of family, community, and tradition. It is a self that seeks the experience of being continually filled up by consuming goods, calories, experiences, politicians, romantic partners, and empathic therapists in an attempt to combat the growing alienation and fragmentation of its era.[3]

A complex system—our consumerist economy—has grown up around this problem, as we have historically continued to go to the same well-worn ruts to try to fill the emptiness.

But there is something even more insidious at work here, which reveals the demonic character of "domination systems" taking on a life of their own and preying on the very people who inhabit those systems. Whole sectors of industry (particularly their propaganda divisions, whether called "marketing" or "advertising") work daily to keep us traveling in these ruts, so as to keep the consumerist economy going and growing, perpetuating the lies about how to fill that emptiness. "This is a powerful illusion. And what fuels the illusion, what impels the individual into this illusion, is the desperation to fill up the empty self."[4] It is in the system's interests to perpetuate the emptiness and promote consumerism as the cure, since the "post-World War II economy . . . is dependent on the continual consumption of nonessential and quickly obsolete items and experiences."[5] Powerful subsystems thus cooperate in the production and maintenance of emptiness in the self, distracting attention and

---

[2] Harvey, *Another City*, 8.
[3] Philip Cushman, "Why the Self Is Empty: Toward a Historically Situated Psychology," *American Psychologist* 45 (1990): 599–611, especially p. 600.
[4] Cushman, "Why the Self is Empty," 606.
[5] Cushman, "Why the Self is Empty," 600.

energy away from those pursuits that might conduce to fullness (and to correcting the sociohistorical factors that have led to our widespread experience of emptiness) for the sake of amassing the wealth that will not fill their members' own emptiness. In this way, consumerist America becomes another example of the sociological dictum, "Each society produces the men [*sic*] it needs" in order for the society, the system, to continue.[6] It also becomes another example of enslavement—of the advertising mogul as much as the shopaholic—to the "powers and principalities," to supra-social forces, the human origins of which are now hidden and whose mandates go unquestioned. John himself came fairly close to this diagnosis in regard to the Christians in Laodicea, whose attempts to make themselves "full" as their non-Christian Laodicean neighbors defined fullness obscured their own awareness of their ongoing emptiness, which could only be filled by participating in an entirely different economy.

Is there an alternative? Following John's method, we would look to the prophets' and Jesus' prescriptions about the acquisition and use of wealth and property, and we might even take the risk of understanding them at face value and living them out. This could *not* be done within the typical social and economic structures of our society, whence Jesus' maxims concerning the impossibility of putting new wine into old wineskins. It would require searching out a new ordering of community that would make it possible to live out those directions regarding wealth and property, sharing and consumption, hence the formation of new wineskins that could contain a new wine—new structures that could support a new way of living. Such a community would embrace practices that prioritized the quest for spiritual, social, and relational progress ("seeking first the kingdom of God and his justice") over the quest for capital and consumer goods. It would prioritize sharing with those in genuine need rather than hoarding or indulging in "impulse buying" or luxury upgrades. It would prioritize the adoption of a lifestyle of simplicity, so as to mobilize more resources to support Christians in prison and distress in restricted nations. Such

---

[6] Peter L. Berger, *Invitation to Sociology: A Humanistic Perspective* (Garden City, NY: Doubleday, 1963), 110.

a community would confront the "world taken for granted" with a striking alternative and raise the possibility of critical examination, questioning, and ultimately rejection in favor of a more hopeful—and more God-centered—alternative. Here we come once again to the importance of *witness* for John, as he calls forth a living witness, a distinctive practice, that not only keeps our own souls clean from Babylon's defilements, but also shakes the people around us out of thinking that "the way things are" is "the way things *must* be," inviting them closer to God's center as well.

Revelation thus invites us into serious dialogue with one another, with our Scriptures as a whole, and with our sisters and brothers across the world over such questions, so that we, too, may find ourselves "standing" before God and the Lamb at their coming. Wrestling together with *these* questions, I'm convinced, means engaging Revelation seriously and discovering what the Spirit is saying to the churches.

Questions for Reflection and Discussion: *John calls for thoroughgoing evaluation of all of the systems of which we are a part and according to whose rules we play in light of God's commands concerning, and vision for, human community. Since this chapter has focused particularly on economics, your evaluation might begin there. (1) What are your own practices of earning, saving, and spending money? What values and beliefs do these practices reflect? (2) What is our society's "wisdom" (from financial advisors to advertising) regarding earning, saving, and spending? (3) What do the Torah, the prophets, Jesus, and the apostles say about earning, saving, and spending? Where do these conflict with society's "wisdom" and your practices? (4) What would have to change in your practices to bring them more in line with God's values and desires for your use of resources? What obstacles, practical and ideological, stand in the way of doing so? (5) What will you do? These questions can be adapted and repeated for any and every facet of your life and the practices of your society: gender roles, violence and war, lines of private and public, the "place" of religion, our relationship to and (ab)use of our environment, the values of self-gratification and self-fulfillment, ad infinitum.*

Chapter 4

LOOKING AT THE IMMEDIATE IN LIGHT OF THE INFINITE: THE SEVEN ORACLES TO THE CHURCHES OF ASIA

We have sought to read Revelation less as a coded text to be interpreted, and more as a text that imposed a Christ-centered interpretation upon the everyday activities, landscapes, and stories encountered by the members of the seven congregations addressed by John in their setting. Having entered the larger picture and the re-picturing of the cosmos as John's Apocalypse was read aloud to the gathered assembly, the hearers are changed, as is their everyday world, which they see anew as but a part of a broader reality that puts the everyday world into a different perspective. The voyeuristic experience of entering into John's encounter with the unseen world—and looking back from there upon the landscape of the visible world—provides a religious experience that disposes hearers indeed to "keep the words of this prophecy" (Rev 22:7) as they return to the normal world where they will hear the Christian prophetess "Jezebel" try to defend her position, encounter further propaganda about the emperor and *Roma Aeterna*, watch goods being transported to ports for transit by ship to Rome, try to engage in their business activities again, and encounter the other everyday realities of their cities. But these figures and activities will hardly look and feel the same, and the hearers will be raising far more critical questions as they move through their lived experience in light of the "wider reality" (and its interpretation of their immediate realities) to which John has exposed them.

In this chapter, we return to the opening segments of Revelation, first to look at where John directs his churches' attention from the very outset, and then to look at the particular issues facing each of the seven churches in their local settings. Throughout the second portion, we will be attentive to how the members of each church will deepen their reading of their own situation as they move from the oracle that addresses them explicitly to hear the whole of Revelation, with the visions of chapters 4–22 continuing to shape their perception of their landscape, its challenges, and their advantageous response.

A Revelation of Jesus Christ

The reader of the seven oracles immediately notices that several challenges face the congregations and elicit John's response: rival prophets eroding the distinctive identity and witness of the group; escalating tension with the synagogue; maintaining witness in the face of increasing suspicion and hostility; and sustaining the spiritual health of particular congregations. Beyond these issues, most disciples would also have been concerned with more mundane challenges, like providing for one's family, negotiating the world of business, or dealing with doubt concerning one's allegiance to this group. John effectively sets *all* of these more immediate crises against the backdrop of a greater, overarching crisis that looms on the horizon. John does this so that his congregations will look at the more immediate challenges ever in light of this greater challenge. This in turn will recommend particular responses to the more immediate crises as the means by which to prepare for, and successfully meet, this greater crisis in regard to which the stakes are greatly elevated. This crisis is *not* the escalation of tension with the host society that John foresees (e.g., in 6:11b; 7:14b; 13:7, 15–17). That is merely a consequence. The crisis is not even the projected political and economic collapse of the empire. *The* critical challenge that must be given attention before all else is the forthcoming visitation of God and God's Messiah.

> John, to the seven churches that are in Asia: Grace and peace to you from the one who is and was and is coming, and from the seven spirits that are before God's throne, and from Jesus Christ—the faithful witness, the firstborn from among the dead,

and the ruler of the kings of the earth. To the one who loves us and freed us from our sins by his blood, who made us a kingdom, priests to his God and Father—to him be glory and power forever and always. Amen.

Look, he is coming with the clouds! Every eye will see him, including those who pierced him, and all the tribes of the earth will mourn because of him. This is so. Amen.

"I am the Alpha and the Omega," says the Lord God, "the one who is and was and is coming, the Almighty." (Rev 1:4–8 CEB)

John describes God at the outset not only as the "one who is and was," but also as "the one who is coming," who is even now on the way (*ho erchomenos*, Rev 1:4, 8), whose intervention in human affairs is imminent. Greeks and Romans used similar language to talk about the eternity of their chief deity, seen, once again, in the acclamation of Zeus: "Zeus was, Zeus is, Zeus shall be; O mighty Zeus!" (Pausanius 10.12.10). John alters this significantly. The picture is no longer of a God who exists in static eternity, but a God who will dynamically encounter God's creation. However much I personally love the hymn, "Holy, Holy, Holy," the hymnwriter got this wrong when he addressed God as the one "which wert and art and evermore shall be"—perhaps "which wert and art and comes victoriously" would more win John's approval.

This dynamic encounter is more dramatically portrayed immediately following the greeting (1:4–6) in a clarion call to pay attention: "Look! He is coming with the clouds; every eye will see him, even those who pierced him; and on his account all the tribes of the earth will wail!" (Rev 1:7 NRSV). John tells his churches to look ahead to an event of universal significance. He amplifies this coming crisis by drawing attention both to the breadth and trauma of its effects—it will evoke "wailing," a response reflecting unpreparedness and failure, from "all earth's tribes." John further amplifies the crisis by drawing attention repeatedly to its imminence both at the outset and at the conclusion of his communication (1:3; 22:7, 12, 20). The greatest threat the hearers face is to be found unprepared to encounter God or God's Christ at his coming (6:12–17), thus being exposed to the threat of the "second death" (2:11) or being written out of the "Book of Life" (3:5). This challenge puts all the others in perspective, subordinates them to itself, and calls Christians to respond to their more immediate crises in the way that will also—and primarily—continue to position them well for encountering the returning Christ. As long as the disciples remained focused on the challenge of their neighbors' pressure, or the challenge of remaining on firm, economical footing, or any other of the everyday challenges that they faced by virtue of being associated with the name of Jesus, they might move toward accommodating to the society around them, since that would generally resolve these challenges. John trumps all these rival foci by placing before the believers' eyes the ultimate crisis, the one most needing to be met successfully. In this way, John steers each disciple to choose the course of action in regard to those everyday challenges that will best align them with "the commandments of God and faithfulness toward Jesus."

But John also draws attention to an even more immediate "coming." One of the greatest surprises of Revelation is that the Lord for whom the disciples watch and wait already walks in the midst of his churches, inspecting, evaluating, preparing to prune away the unfruitful, unfaithful branches or to remove the lampstands whose light fails to burn as it ought. The image of Christ walking "among the seven gold lampstands" that represent the churches (Rev 1:20; 2:1) presents an even more immediate threat to congregations that have not kept faith with him.

And Christ now looks nothing like he did when he walked by the shores of the Sea of Galilee or through the streets of Jerusalem.

> I turned to see who was speaking to me, and when I turned, I saw seven oil lamps burning on top of seven gold stands. In the middle of the lampstands I saw someone who looked like the Son of Man. He wore a robe that stretched down to his feet, and he had a gold sash around his chest. His head and hair were white as white wool—like snow—and his eyes were like a fiery flame. His feet were like fine brass that has been purified in a furnace, and his voice sounded like rushing water. He held seven stars in his right hand, and from his mouth came a sharp, two-edged sword. His appearance was like the sun shining with all its power. When I saw him, I fell at his feet like a dead man. But he put his right

hand on me and said, "Don't be afraid. I'm the first and the last, and the living one. I was dead, but look! Now I'm alive forever and always. I have the keys of Death and the Grave." (1:12–18 CEB modified)

The Lord, now glorified beyond death, is far more powerful, awe-inspiring, and divine than even the most impressive alabaster statues of the Roman emperor, glowing in the smoky light of the oil lamps in the imperial temples, or than the most elaborate costumes and accessories could ever make the living emperor appear. Unless the congregations fall in line swiftly with his righteous demands (recovering their former love and their former commitment to avoid every semblance of idolatrous worship), Christ's immediacy threatens swift judgment with no need to wait for the second coming:

"I will come to you and remove your lampstand from its place, unless you repent." (2:5 NRSV)

"Repent then. If not, I will come to you soon and make war against them with the sword of my mouth." (2:16 NRSV)

"I am throwing her on a bed, and those who commit adultery with her I am throwing into great distress, unless they repent of her doings; and I will strike her children dead. And all the churches will know that I am the one who searches minds and hearts, and I will give to each of you as your works deserve." (2:22–23 NRSV)

At the same time, however, if one is disposed to heed Jesus' summons, his presence in the midst of the churches signifies the immediacy of help and fellowship. The oracle to Laodicea, appropriately the last of the series of seven, closes the distance between the congregations and Christ even further—the one who throughout the oracles declares that he is coming arrives, here, at the very threshold: "See! I stand at the door and knock!" (Rev 3:20). Whether for judgment or strengthening, then, Christians must come to terms at once with the glorified Christ who stands at the door. John guides the churches to see that their response to Christ's exhortations to single-hearted discipleship will determine whether they encounter him there as judge and executioner, or as a welcome guest.

It is not difficult to discern what John would say to us through the opening chapter of his Revelation, for it remains essentially the same as his challenge to his own congregations.

If, with John, we keep "the day of the wrath of God and of the Lamb" before our eyes, what we must decide to do *this* day, and how we must respond to each new presenting situation, becomes that much clearer.

If, with John, we know Jesus as "the ruler of the kings of the earth" and as the "one who loves us and freed us from our sins by his blood, who made us a kingdom, priests to his God and Father," our primary identity will be rooted in our place in the kingdom of God, which we share with the redeemed from every people, tribe, nation, and language group. It will not be rooted in some national or political body constructed by human beings and their party lines. Our primary allegiance will be to this One Lord and One God in every aspect of our lives, out of gratitude for our costly redemption and in acknowledgment that we have been made part of a very real political entity whose head is Christ.

If, with John, we know Jesus not as he was when he walked the roads of Palestine, but as he is now that he has entered into a transformed existence beyond all mortal experience, we will know the awesome majesty of the One whom we worship, and in whose name we go forth to serve as "priests" (Rev 1:6; 5:10). This will give us courage, as it gave John and as he hoped it would give his congregations, to confront evil and oppression in families, businesses, and governments, to relieve the needs of the suffering, and to bear witness to God's way of ordering a just and humane society, not in fear of the overshadowing powers of the Enemy, but in confidence in the triumph of the Christ who sits at God's right hand, invested with God's power, and who is coming to bring justice to "every tribe, language, people, and nation." He who is the beginning and the ending will always have the last word over all who oppose God's righteous reign.

And John would also have us, as we prepare to meet him at his coming, alert to find the glorified Christ already standing in the midst of his churches affirming our works of faith, confronting our compromise, and encouraging our renewed devotion. Thus John calls us to be prepared to encounter Jesus as he walks in our midst, and to be mindful of the urgency of responding to what this Jesus would tell us, since by means of such response we might indeed avoid being left in a position to wail at his return.

What the Spirit says to the churches

The seven oracles to the seven churches are probably among the more frequently preached-upon passages in Revelation, and therefore among the more familiar. I say "oracles," again, rather than "letters" because, in fact, each communication to a congregation begins with a variant of the prophetic oracle formula "Thus says the Lord," as in "These things says the One who holds the seven stars." "To the angel of the church in Asia, write.. . ." is not a variation of the letter-opening formula, but a command to John the visionary to record the oracle that follows. These oracles are favorite texts for preaching since pastors rightly intuit that reflecting on what Jesus commended and censured in these churches can help us diagnose what Jesus would commend and censure in our churches.

These seven oracles follow a formulaic pattern, with only a few variations:

1. Jesus identifies himself as the one speaking, usually reminding the congregation of some significant facet of his identity, power, or achievement;

2. Jesus identifies what the particular congregation being addressed has been doing well, and encourages and honors them for this;

3. Jesus identifies where the congregation, or some portion thereof, has fallen short of a discerning, wholehearted response of faithfulness, and challenges them to give their energies and attention to remedying these deficiencies; and

4. Jesus warns the congregation of the consequences of failing to invest themselves in constructive change in these areas, and encourages them with the positive consequences of taking his diagnosis and admonitions to heart.

John gives a number of clues that he expects his hearers to meditate on these prophetic oracles to their congregations in light of the whole of Revelation—reinforcing, incidentally, my primary thesis that Revelation as a whole, and not just these opening oracles, was written with *them* in mind, and not us. For example, while the images Jesus uses to identify himself are almost all drawn from John initial vision of Jesus in chapter 1, many of the warnings and promises involve images that are only explained later in the visions. The "tree of life which is in the paradise of God" (2:7), the threat of the "second death" (2:11), Jesus "making war with the sword of [his] mouth" (2:16), the role of the "Book of Life" and being "clothed in white robes" (3:5), being inscribed in "the New Jerusalem that comes down from my God" (3:12), and sharing Jesus' authority upon thrones (3:27) all look ahead to the actions and scenes of Revelation 7 and 19–22. As we examine a selection of these oracles, then, we will also give attention to their reinforcement or further illumination in light of the material in Revelation that precedes and follows.

Smyrna

> Write this to the angel of the church in Smyrna:
>
> These are the words of the one who is the first and the last, who died and came back to life: I know your hardship and poverty (though you are actually rich). I also know the hurtful things that have been spoken about you by those who say they are Jews (though they are not, but are really Satan's synagogue). Don't be afraid of what you are going to suffer. Look! The devil is going to throw some of you into prison in order to test you. You will suffer hardship for ten days. Be faithful even to the point of death, and I will give you the crown of life. If you can hear, listen to what the Spirit is saying to the churches. Those who emerge victorious won't be hurt by the second death. (2:8–11 CEB)

Breaking the general pattern of the oracles, there is no word of rebuke for this congregation. The church whose situation is the most miserable is most honored in Christ's eyes!

The oracle identifies three important issues in the life of this congregation: first, their material poverty; second, the hostility between the church and the local synagogue; and third, the likelihood of social pressure escalating to martyrdom in the near future. The cause of the Christians' poverty in this city is not made explicit, but we do know that John is intensely concerned that Christians not profit from the Roman imperial economy, since he regards the system itself as an entangling web of injustice and exploitation. The Smyrnaean Christians have clearly avoided this. But we might surmise further that their poverty comes from their refusal to do what it takes to maintain business networks in a pagan city, and from their neighbors' increasing alienation from them because of their changed lifestyle. Economic embargo could be a powerful, unofficial tool to let deviants know you don't approve of their new behaviors. Thus their temporal poverty is a consequence of their obedience to God's call, which has otherwise made them rich in Christ's estimation.

The issue of the level of persecution facing this congregation and the other churches is an important one, all the more as most every thumbnail sketch of the setting of Revelation claims that John was writing to comfort churches that are suffering severe persecution. A close look at the text suggests that we need a much more nuanced view. It is certainly true that the non-Christians were suspicious of, and often hostile to, the early Christian movement. The kinds of harassment that *some* of the Christians addressed by John currently experienced might have been limited to verbal assaults ("slander," 2:9), economic hardship ("poverty," 2:9), and other indignities to be "endured" (2:3, 19). Insults, physical abuse, and disenfranchisement were the common lot of many Christians throughout the Eastern Mediterranean (see Heb 10:32–34; 13:3; 1 Pet 2:11–12, 18–25; 3:13–17; 4:1–4, 12–19; 1 Thess 3:1–6; 2 Thess 1:3–9). Such harassment communicated a message: the Christians' neighbors were calling this deviant minority group to fall in line again with the values and behaviors considered important for the larger society's well-being—particularly to return to the traditional piety upon which all other social values were founded, and to the solidarity and civic unity that such piety expressed and facilitated. This call, no doubt, weighed heavily on the minds of many Christians, pushing them to think about how to balance the human drive to enjoy a serene and secure life with their religious commitments to the God of Israel and his Messiah. John also knew that continued resistance to their neighbors' summons would eventuate in heavier-handed attempts on society's part to address the problem of deviants in their midst, filling up the tally of the martyrs (6:11). John had no illusions about the consequences of his preferred course of action.

Martyrdom, however, was in fact quite rare in the first century. It usually affected leaders rather than the general membership. Rome appears not to have gone looking for Christians to prosecute, even in the early second century. It was local rather than empire-wide. Even when Nero scapegoated the Christians in Rome for the great fire in 64 C.E., Nero's actions were limited to the Roman Christian community in connection with a specific crime—arson—and did not become a precedent for the treatment of Christians. While John remembers that many Christians have died under Roman rule, seen for example in the souls of the martyrs under the altar, John can name only one near-contemporary martyr from the seven churches—Antipas of Pergamum. And we know nothing of the circumstances of his death, whether it was the result of official proceedings or a back-alley lynching. There is also no Roman record of Domitian's having taken any actions against Christians throughout the empire, though he was responsible for executing several high-ranking Roman converts in the capital itself on the charge of "atheism."

Even more problematic for John are those congregations that seem to coexist all too peaceably with their neighbors in the shadow of Rome. There is not a hint that the Christians in Sardis and Laodicea have experienced rejection by their neighbors. Indeed, the indictment of these churches appears to stem from the fact that they blend in all too well and mingle all too effectively with the partners of Rome and worshipers of idols all around them. As we think about the diversity of the congregations John addresses, we should always bear in mind that John is equally interested in comforting the afflicted and afflicting the comfortable.

John does see in Antipas, however, the shape of things to come if Christians continue in their bold witness as did Antipas.

This death shows Christians just how precarious their position is, and why muting their Christian witness rather than trumpeting their allegiance to Jesus might be the more advantageous course. Such witness criticized the heart of the empire and could not help but provoke a strong, allergic response among those who, as partners of the whore, looked to that empire for security and even prosperity (we could look to his vision of the model two witnesses in chapter 11, for example). The scenes of marginalization and martyrdom that dominate the visions are mostly visions for the near future, not of John's present, and history proved John to be correct. Not fifteen years later, Christians in the neighboring province of Bithynia would be faced with the choice: offer incense and a splash of wine to the emperor Trajan and the other gods, or be executed for your stubbornness, if for nothing else (Pliny, *Epistles* 10.96–97). After this, the precedent would spread the practice.

This is what John announces will be the case for the Christians in Smyrna. It is evident that hostility between the church and the synagogue went both ways. When John calls them "a synagogue of Satan" (2:9; see also 3:9), he is exhibiting the same kind of name-calling that we find in other situations where very closely related groups have arguments with one another. In the Fourth Gospel, Jesus denounces opposing Jewish leaders as the spawn of Satan (John 8:44), and the Jewish sect at Qumran referred to other Jews outside their group as the "congregation of Beliar" (1QH 2:22; 1QM 4:9). But John's label, "synagogue of Satan," may reflect more than a stock slur. In Revelation, Satan is the force behind the Principate and the imperial cult. The worship and authority of the emperor is grounded in the worship and authority of Satan. When John's audience looks for Satan in their context, John leads them to look toward Zeus—that divine force supporting the rule of Rome through her emperors in the dominant cultural ideology.

The Jewish people were, on the whole, very careful to observe the first commandment and avoid any entanglements with idolatrous cults. A recent development in their history, however, may have won John's enduring censure. The Jews had formerly expressed their loyalty to the emperors by offering sacrifices in their temple on the emperor's behalf, exempting

Jews everywhere from showing loyalty by participating in sacrifices *to* the emperor. After the temple's destruction in 70 C.E., however, a new sign of loyalty was imposed upon Judeans. The temple tax, formerly paid by every adult Jew for the support of the daily sacrifices and maintenance of the Jerusalem temple, would now be collected on behalf of the Temple of Jupiter Capitolinus in Rome (Josephus, *J.W.* 7.6.6, §218). The price of toleration was an annual contribution to a pagan cult—indeed, *the* pagan cult—literally taking what belonged to God and giving it to Caesar. [Fig. 4.1 and 4.2, see p. 64.] This practice allowed local Jewish communities to continue to flourish in the Roman economy and enjoy legal toleration within the empire. It might have seemed a reasonable compromise, and indeed a sign of Rome's leniency after the Jewish Revolt. But, for the impractical and uncompromising prophet on Patmos, his fellow Jews had compromised their witness and loyalty to the One God by their willingness to give the tribute due to the One, True God to the central religious site of the Roman anti-God, putting them in league with Satan.

On the other side, the synagogue's "slander" of the Christians is also intelligible against the backdrop of Jewish communities living in the situation post-70 C.E. Christian claims about the meaning of the Jewish Scriptures, the identity of the people of God, and the role of the Torah in the people of God were problematic for other Jews from the beginning. After the suppression of the First Jewish Revolt, however, Jews would be even more interested in distancing themselves from a group whose leader had been crucified as a revolutionary, a group that eagerly awaited his return to finish what he started. Monitoring boundaries closely, pointing out that Christians were not Jews, would help maintain good relations with both Roman officials and their own business associates. By dissociating themselves from the Christians, the synagogue set in motion an investigation that would expose the disciples as a potentially subversive group that, when examined, would be subjected to penal action, since it was becoming clear that the Christian movement did not enjoy the official toleration afforded Jews.

John prepares the believers in Smyrna for a coming sifting. Some of them will be examined and face execution. In the

Roman system, imprisonment was not a form of punishment. Rather, it was used to detain defendants awaiting trial, to gain the cooperation of recalcitrant parties, and to hold till their execution those sentenced to death, hence the call to "be faithful unto death" in this situation. The Smyrnean Christians will find much in the later visions to resonate with their situation. The official proceedings they are about to face are one instance of Satan's determination to make war with the sisters and brothers of the divine child who was caught up into heaven, namely, Jesus himself (12:17), which Satan would accomplish through the instruments of Roman jurisprudence. The local trials they faced were but one manifestation of an empire-wide trial facing the entire brotherhood and sisterhood. They would be encouraged in the face of their material poverty as they considered the corruption and defilement that infused the economy of Babylon (ch. 18). They would see themselves in the companies of victors who overcame Satan's trials, who wear the wreaths of victory through fidelity unto death (7:13–17; 15:1–4; 20:4–6). They would see the "second death" that threatened all who compromised their faithfulness to the One God, from which they would be forever safe after their steadfastness (14:9–11; 20:11–15). Of course, they had Jesus' own assurance, who had himself shown the way to overcome by displaying fidelity unto death, and was indeed living proof that death was only the beginning.

Pergamum and Thyatira

Write this to the angel of the church in Pergamum:

These are the words of the one who has the sharp, two-edged sword: I know that you are living right where Satan's throne is. You are holding on to my name, and you didn't break faith with me even at the time that Antipas, my faithful witness, was killed among you, where Satan lives. But I have a few things against you, because you have some there who follow Balaam's teaching. Balaam had taught Balak to trip up the Israelites so that they would eat food sacrificed to idols and commit sexual immorality. In the same way, you have some who follow the Nicolaitans' teaching. So change your hearts and lives. If you don't, I am coming to you soon, and I will make war on them with the sword that comes from my mouth. If you can hear, listen to what the Spirit is saying to the churches. I will give those who emerge victorious some of the hidden manna to eat. I will also give to each of them a white stone with a new name written on it, which no one knows except the one who receives it. (2:12–17 CEB)

We have already addressed the issue of the hostility of the Pergamene Christians' neighbors and the death of Antipas, the lone-named martyr from the seven churches. The major issue facing this congregation concerns the "Gospel" of the Nicolaitans. This is also the major issue John raises in the congregation in Thyatira, where a particular Christian prophetess also preaches a problematic gospel:

I have this against you: you put up with that woman, Jezebel, who calls herself a prophet. You allow her to teach and to mislead my servants into committing sexual immorality and eating food sacrificed to idols. I gave her time to change her heart and life, but she refuses to change her life of prostitution. Look! I'm throwing her onto a sickbed. I am casting those who have committed adultery with her into terrible hardship—if they don't change their hearts from following her practices—and I will even put her children to death with disease. (2:20–23 CEB)

All that John tells us about these rival teachers is that they lead Christians "to eat things sacrificed to idols and to have illicit sexual relations" (2:14–15, 20). Whatever this may mean, this much is clear: the rival teachers try to make room for Christians to interact more closely with their non-Christian neighbors where pagan rites are concerned.

Where would people eat food sacrificed to idols, and why would an inner-Christian movement seek to render such action defensible? Public religious festivals were frequently occasions for social feasting, opportunities to celebrate the solidarity enjoyed between citizenry and gods. One would also encounter "food sacrificed to idols" at private dinner parties or at dinners of clubs and associations (including "trade guilds"), which involved rites paying honor to the patron god or goddess and, increasingly, to the emperor as an antidote to any suspicion against such clubs. Associations of those sharing a common trade, while not serving the same functions as unions today, nevertheless provided important opportunities for networking, offered a stable circle of social relationships, and often formed something of a safety net in times of hardship (as when an association would provide for the burial of members in need). The person who sought to avoid any idolatrous rite and any food that had been "consecrated" by such a rite would have to withdraw from a great many important social and business settings, with serious social and economic consequences.

The "Nicolaitans" and "Jezebel" were promoting an understanding of Christian practice that would allow Christians to participate in those social, civic, and perhaps even religious contexts where food sacrificed to idols would be ingested. Such flexibility would alleviate a great deal of social tension between church and society and open up the doors once again to those networks that facilitated survival, even thriving.

John doesn't tell us how Jezebel or the Nicolaitans argued their case, but neither was this the first time Christians sought a more moderate approach to the question of idolatry. This very issue figured large in Corinth, to judge from 1 Corinthians, decades before. Perhaps the Nicolaitans, too, argued that since "an idol is nothing" and "there is no God but the One" (1 Cor 8:4), ingesting meat that had been offered to an idol could not bring spiritual harm to the disciple. They might have remembered the saying of Jesus that "there is nothing outside a person that, by going in, is able to defile him or her" (Mark 7:15). Why, then, should Christians—to their own hurt and impoverishment—provoke their neighbors unnecessarily by remaining absent from civic festivals and from dinners in the homes of their associates or the dining halls where their patrons and others would hold symposia? While the Christians would still know that "an idol is nothing," their neighbors would no longer think of them as atheists, or as antisocial and therefore potentially subversive.

For John, however, the pressing question was not "How far can we go to foster good relations with our non-Christian neighbors and to provide for our own social and economic security?" For him, the question was "How clear can we be in our witness that the worship of any God but the One is absolutely wrong?" Where the Nicolaitans' compromise was adopted, Christians would no longer by their blatant practice confront their neighbors with claims about the reality of One God and the exclusive honors due that God. They would no longer witness against the empty pretensions of Roman imperial ideology, especially as enshrined in the cult of Augustus and *Roma*. And, we recall, John was also more allergic than his rival prophets to participating at all in an economic system that required the acknowledgment of other gods—and this on top of its already self-serving and exploitative practices.

John accuses these rival teachers of loosening sexual morals as well. While some take this literally, I have doubts that John meant that they were leading people into "committing fornication" in a literal sense. Yes, parties in the Greco-Roman world *could* get out of hand, and perhaps that's one reason college fraternities still bear Greek letters above their doors. But John picks up this language from the story of Balaam in Numbers. Balaam masterminded the Midianites' plan to lead the people of Israel into worshiping their gods and assimilating with their people, which involved Midianite women seducing Israelite men (Num 25:1–2; 31:16). John wants his audience to look at the Nicolaitans as another Balaam in their midst, leading them to assimilate and, in the process, break faith with the One God (with disastrous consequences). Moreover, John will talk about sexual intercourse and about partnerships, whether with a whore or as a bride, throughout Revelation in ways that clearly have a figurative meaning. "Sexual immorality" functions as a label for all improper intercourse with Roman society and its gods; sexual purity or fidelity represents loyalty to the one God and God's Messiah. In a visionary world in which Roman imperial power and economy are portrayed as a great prostitute (in Greek, *pornē*), the metaphorical implications of "leading my servants to commit fornication" (in Greek, *porneia*) are easy to catch: the Nicolaitans and, in the neighboring city, Jezebel are teaching that one can make some room for idolatry in order to "get into bed" with the brokers of power and wealth around them.

John reminds the Pergamene Christians exactly what power stands ultimately behind all idolatrous ritual: Satan and his demons. The people around them may not "stop worshipping demons and idols made of gold, silver, bronze, stone, and wood" (9:20), but do the Christians themselves really want to be associated with those practices in light of the day of Christ's appearing? And the Pergamenes live in the city where Satan has his very throne, according to this oracle, where it is mentioned twice for emphasis (2:13). While notable scholars have read this as a reference to Pergamum's Temple of *Roma et Augusti*, the city's most distinctive landmark was the great Altar of Zeus, set atop a mountain from which it dominated the city (and, indeed, had the appearance of a great marble throne). Writing of this throne-like altar, Colin Hemer observed that "the obsessive serpent motif of its sculptures and the title 'Soter'," "Savior," applied to Zeus, would "signal to John deliberate parody of Christ and the cult's being in league with Satan."[1] The identification of Satan as the spiritual force *behind* the imperial power (the many-headed sea-beast) throughout the visions strongly suggests that the "throne of Satan" would reflect some landmark or practice associated more closely with the traditional gods, especially the chief god, Zeus.

John's visions will make the Pergamenes look at many of their local landmarks differently. Their fellow citizens flocked to the sacrifices at the temples of Athena, Demeter, and Dionysus, but John invites the Christians to see this as the worship of Satan's underlings by deceived and deviant souls (9:20–21). Their fellow citizens took special pride in the activities of the Temple of *Roma* and Augustus that had brought them regional recognition as *neōkoros*, a pride that would escalate in the coming decades with the construction of the new Temple of Trajan, but this was all a manifestation of the deception of Satan and his local agent on the land (13:11–18). How, then, could the Nicolaitans actually be *helping* by making room for Christians to edge back toward those settings, when they should be fleeing them entirely?

Formerly, the Pergamene Christians, like those in the other cities, would have been continually overwhelmed by the sight of the majority who did not hold to their commitments, who tried to impress upon the Christians that *they* were the deviant ones who needed to get in line. After seeing the whole picture

---

[1]Colin Hemer, *The Letters to the Seven Churches of Asia in Their Local Setting* (Sheffield: JSOT Press, 1986), 186–91.

again, radiating out from the throne of the One God, the tables are turned. The visions of angels and archangels, of all the company of heaven, and of creation itself lauding God and the Lamb (4:1–5, 11) assure the Christians that they are *not* the deviant ones, *not even* the minority report. Formerly, these believers might have allowed themselves to drink in something of the party line about the golden age that Rome restored; now they are remembering the undertones to the "official" ideology of the Roman Peace.

John also paints the prophetess whom he calls "Jezebel" in Babylon's scarlet hues, particularly in regard to "sexual immorality": Jezebel teaches other Christians to "fornicate" (2:20) and has not herself repented "of her fornication" (2:21); Babylon disseminates her defilement through "the wine of the passion of her fornication" (14:8). These verbal associations reinforce John's warning that Jezebel's ministry leads believers into the webs of impure entanglements spun by Rome, with the result that they will incur a share of responsibility for the injustices of Roman imperialism, for the sake of the temporal benefits partnership brings (18:4). Particularly after experiencing John's visions, getting in bed with Rome would not look nearly so attractive.

As the Pergamene (and Thyatiran) Christians read their situation in light of Revelation, they are likely to conclude with John that survival is not a matter of developing a theology that allows for us to eat food sacrificed to idols and to form entangling alliances with the Roman order. It is a matter of bearing bold and uncompromising witness to the One, True God in the midst of the worship of many false gods, of putting one's hope in the coming kingdom of God's Messiah rather than the *Pax Romana*, and coming out from, and keeping oneself unstained by, Babylon's worldwide web of exploitation.

Laodicea

Write this to the angel of the church in Laodicea:

These are the words of the Amen, the faithful and true witness, the ruler [or "beginning"] of God's creation. I know your works.

You are neither cold nor hot. I wish that you were either cold or hot. So because you are lukewarm, and neither hot nor cold, I'm about to spit you out of my mouth. After all, you say, 'I'm rich, and I've grown wealthy, and I don't need a thing.' You don't realize that you are miserable, pathetic, poor, blind, and naked. My advice is that you buy gold from me that has been purified by fire so that you may be rich, and white clothing to wear so that your nakedness won't be shamefully exposed, and ointment to put on your eyes so that you may see. I correct and discipline those whom I love. So be earnest and change your hearts and lives. Look! I'm standing at the door and knocking. If any hear my voice and open the door, I will come in to be with them, and will have dinner with them, and they will have dinner with me. As for those who emerge victorious, I will allow them to sit with me on my throne, just as I emerged victorious and sat down with my Father on his throne. If you can hear, listen to what the Spirit is saying to the churches. (3:14–22 CEB)

One often hears "hot" interpreted as "fervent" in faith while "cold" represents those who are completely indifferent to Christ. Such interpretations are entirely speculative (not to mention implausible, for Chirst would not command fervent faithfulness and complete indifference equally).

The oracle, however, does not call for the interpretation of what "hot" and "cold" would precisely represent, only for the interpretation of "lukewarmness." The audience had plenty of experience with waters of different temperatures. Laodicea, which received water via an aqueduct from a distance, had a tepid and nauseating water supply in contrast to neighboring Colossae's cold water or Hierapolis's hot springs. Moreover, both hot and cold water would be served at banquets, with tepid water being offered as an emetic between courses (hence the connection between the church's lukewarmness and Christ's vomiting them out of his mouth). Those who understand both "hot" and "cold" to label positive qualities, rather than fervor on the one hand and complete indifference on the other, are on firmer ground. This would better reflect the uses of cold and hot water in the first-century social context in general and the local setting of Laodicea in particular: for example, Hierapolis's hot water is healing and salutary; the cold water from Colossae's springs is also welcoming and refreshing.

Water that is lukewarm is "room temperature." It has completely adapted to its surroundings and taken on its quality, such that it no longer exhibits a healthful and welcome contrast. So it is with the Laodicean Christians, who think no differently from other citizens of Laodicea profiting from the economic boom of trade in the imperial period. The proud but deceived person who says "But I am rich and need nothing" is known also from philosophical texts and from the Hebrew prophets. What should scare the wits into the Laodicean Christians, however, is to discover that they are thinking very much like Babylon herself:

> "In her heart she says, 'I sit like a queen! I'm not a widow. I'll never see grief.' This is why her plagues will come in a single day—deadly disease, grief, and hunger. She will be consumed by fire because the Lord God who judges her is powerful." (Rev 18:7–8 CEB)

The wealth and plenty of the Roman economy is deceptive: it gives Rome false confidence in its security, a false confidence easily passed along to its partners, among whom the Laodicean Christians dangerously find themselves. They are probably caught most between the eyes when, later in the visions, the voice of Christ speaks again: "Look! I'm coming like a thief! Favored are those who stay awake and clothed so that they don't go around naked and exposed to shame" (Rev 16:15 CEB). Like Babylon herself, they are in danger of having their true nakedness—their true poverty and false pride—exposed to their shame, even to their ultimate loss. With Christ's summons to them to buy clothing from him to cover their shame, John has disposed them to listen carefully when he speaks of robes being given out, and to discern what changes in practice will be necessary to be found clothed in the white robes of Christ's loyal and courageous witnesses when Christ comes, so as to stand before him with confidence rather than cry out to the hills to cover them, and hide them from the searching eyes of God and the Lamb.

Listening for what the Spirit is saying to the churches

The pattern observed in these oracles offers itself as a guide for meditation and study not only focused on the oracles themselves, or on Revelation as a whole, but on the whole counsel of Scripture as we seek illumination from outside our situation on our situation:

- What do we most need to bear in mind about Jesus, in order to respond to him and to our particular situation in a manner that is fully invested?

- What are we doing that bears effective witness (in our speech, in our deeds, in our relationships) to the Creator God and to Jesus the Redeemer, such that we hear Christ's word of commendation?

- What are we doing, or failing to do, such that this witness is stifled, muted, or betrayed?

- Where is our loyalty, our zeal, our full-blooded response to Jesus found wanting?

- What promises from God do we need to keep before our eyes in order to change for the better and respond as would please Christ as he stands in our midst?

But, as John placed the answers to such questions for his own congregations within a thoroughgoing interpretation of their world in the light of God's purposes and just requirements of his creation, so John would call us to do the same—to seek the same "apocalyptic adjustment" to our view of the world that he sought and gave to his congregations. Revelation still interprets—and calls us to interpret—the social, political, religious, and economic realities of our everyday experience. It does so not by asking us to equate its images with those realities, playing the endless game of "pin the tail on the antichrist" or trying to line up the seven seals with the broadcasts on CNN or rezoning such-and-such a nation as the real "Babylon." Rather, Revelation invites Christ-followers into the same processes that guided John as he came upon his own "apocalyptic adjustment" to the way he looked at and evaluated the world around him, and was thus enabled to communicate this to his congregations, calling them to ever greater levels of covenant faithfulness toward God and the Lamb.

The product of John's engagements—Revelation itself—suggests that his process would commend, at least, the following steps to those who would continue to wrestle alongside him to see their world beyond the blinders of their social location, so as to speak prophetically within and from that location.

Immerse yourselves in Scripture

John *lived* in the Hebrew Scriptures. John saw his world in the light of those Scriptures, under which the powers of the world and the practices of the church were all measured in the balance, found wanting, and challenged to close the distance (or, at the very least, indicted for the distance). John was a true steward of the tradition. He was not progressive. He was not practical. He was not adaptive. He did not cater to contemporary trends. There was no room for compromise. But it was John's commitment as a bond-servant to the tradition of Israel and of Jesus that enabled him to break free from the power of the lies of the domination systems into which he and his hearers had been born and bred, and to break their hold over himself and his congregations. These traditions opened his eyes to Roman imperialism in a way that was not possible for a Jezebel or a member of the Nicolaitan circle or most of the Christians in Laodicea, and gave him a language by means of which to invite others into that liberation from the matrix of Roman imperial propaganda.

Immersing ourselves in the world of Scripture, we run the same risk and we reach for the same prize. We run the risk of being rebuffed as outdated fossils or relics. But we also are given a space in which we can live outside of the values, priorities, and stories of the dominant culture that surrounds us, with its idolization of power, wealth, and self-gratification, and outside of our own stories with the longings, struggles, and distractions they impose upon us. We are a given a place where all of these things loosen their hold on us, and from which we can look back at all these things from a different perspective, one that puts them *in* perspective and empowers us to encounter them as people who will "keep the commandments of God and the faith of Jesus" (Rev 14:12).

Immerse yourselves in prayer and meditation

The encounter with the tradition of the prophets and apostles is vital, but equally vital is the encounter with the living God, which brings that tradition to life and causes it to speak a living word to us, about us, and through us. And, frankly, Revelation challenges us to entertain a greater openness toward entering into alternate states of consciousness, where God's Spirit can speak to our spirits and consciousness more directly, piecing together what we have gathered from the sacred texts and seen in our lives and the world around us. If we frequent the world of the Scriptures and the heritage of the Christian tradition fully and often, we will be able to exercise appropriate discernment, testing everything and holding on to what is good.

Center yourselves on God and the Lamb

The path into God's presence remains the discipline of worship and adoration, in the company of the hosts of heaven and of the faithful on earth. John invited his hearers to enter into the scenes of worship, to find themselves centered on God and the Lamb, and to find their way through the challenges of life in Roman Asia without compromising their God-centered orbit. Entering into worship and letting worship change you, your sense of reality, and your whole orientation to everyday life, is an essential facet of the apocalyptic adjustment that Revelation nurtures. It is important to qualify this, however, by saying that a "worship service" is not the same as "worship." A worship service fits into the realities of Monday through Saturday (and may even be dull by comparison), but worship puts one in touch with the realities that change Monday through Saturday. Entering into this kind of genuine worship is not as simple as choosing one music style over another, or seeking one emotional effect rather than another. Indeed, where the conversation centers on these externals, people seeking life-changing worship are barking up the wrong tree entirely. Rather, it involves becoming so fully aware of God's presence, character, and power that worship is the natural response of ourselves and those around us.

Examine public discourse

John knew the power that stories have over the lives of individuals. We seek contexts for our lives, broader contexts that will give them meaning. Domination systems are happy to supply those stories and those hopes that will give us meaning and context, though in such a way as secures our allegiance—even our servitude—to those systems at the same time.

Revelation suggests three other important contexts—the context of the sacred tradition, the context of gathered worship, and the context of prayer and meditation in the presence of God—in which to locate ourselves and from which to examine the "stories" that representatives of domination systems tell, and have told for decades or centuries, the stories into which we have been born. What is the impact upon us, or what are the feelings and inclinations evoked by, the story of America's rise and exercise of sovereignty? How is this story evoked in the context of our political and economic initiatives here and throughout the world? As we immerse ourselves in *God's* story and God's conversation more fully, in what ways do we begin to hear our nation's story differently, or see its policies and strategies differently? Revelation demands of us that we raise such questions in regard to our own national ideologies, whatever countries we hail from.

Exercise vigilance

John watched and critiqued Roman imperialism globally and in its local manifestations in Asia Minor, but he also kept open a critical ear and eye within the Christian communities. The contexts of Scripture, prayer, and worship—in concert with our prophetic critique of the "spirit of the age" nurtured by the powers around us—position us to exercise more effective vigilance within our own congregations. Part of the ongoing charge of disciples entrusted with any kind of leadership in the church is to keep listening for the Spirit's word concerning things being done well, things being overlooked, things taking a turn away from radical faithfulness, and forthcoming opportunities to bear living testimony to God's love, mercy, righteousness, and value, striving to discern these things in light of the "bigger picture" of who God is, what God wants, and the direction in which God is driving human history.

Redraw the maps

Revelation moves us to think beyond our national borders and consider the global community, redrawing our mental maps of "us" and "them" in light of the larger map of God's reign extending from the center of the cosmos in God's throne room out through and over "every kinship group and language group and people and race" (Rev 5:7). Revelation opens up our minds to the possibility of thinking beyond the terms of national borders—boundaries that the dominant ideologies of this world have engraved deeply into our hearts. In so doing, it opens us up to a global perspective on the church and to the perspectives of our sisters and brothers across the globe upon our own witness within our own nation. Once again, we often depend upon the perspectives of people from outside our native systems even to have the opportunity to reflect critically upon those systems and their impact on people inside and outside of the same.

Dare to see

John's example challenges us to dare to see things as they really are—that is, to see more of our setting than the domination systems at work would want us to see. John challenges us to look at the costs in human terms of perpetuating those systems and to look beyond the public discourse that tends to hide that which would make us uncomfortable with our ongoing participation in and alongside those systems. John challenges us, positively, also to dare to see things as they could be where God is truly worshiped, his commandments lived out, and the testimony of Jesus re-embodied.

Revelation is a visionary text. We are perhaps most true to it when we, too, engage in constructing visions that capture the ideals communicated by God. When I first saw the bumper sticker that reads "Visualize world peace," I thought this to be an insipid response to the realities of violence and hatred. But the more I thought about it, the more I was convinced that those who are able to dream, to visualize a state of affairs where war, violence, prejudice, and poverty are no more—truly to "see" the alternative—can never again devote their gifts and services to anything but bringing that vision into reality. Perhaps this is why the prophet Joel linked dreaming dreams and seeing visions to the activity of God's Holy Spirit—what else could possibly stand behind an activity that could change the world! Revelation closes our scriptural canon, but not without first opening us up to the task of the seer, the visionary, who calls us beyond the second-rate state of affairs we all too often accept as "reality."

Dare to set your hopes in God's future

Revelation still speaks about the future and makes us look at the present in light of that future. The "mystery of God" is not yet fulfilled; the kingdoms of this world have not yet surrendered to God and God's Christ. The marriage of the Bride and the Lamb has not yet been celebrated, and death, sorrow, and the curse still weigh upon our hearts. Revelation is thus also a book of longing, of desire, of hope—a longing that echoes through our churches most clearly in the season of Advent, which, traditionally, not only reminisces about Christ's first coming, but also calls Christians to prepare for his coming again. The hymns of the church point us to our great need of God's redemption and for the mystery of God to be fulfilled. As John prays, "Come, Lord Jesus," so we pray, "O come, O come, Emmanuel." As John shows us the destiny to which

God leads us, we sing with great longing: "Bid thou our sad divisions cease, and be thyself our King of Peace; make safe the way that leads on high, and close the path to misery." And just as Revelation arouses those longings, it assures the pilgrims of the certainty of the satisfaction of those desires in the plan and sovereignty of the God of history: "Rejoice! Rejoice! Emmanuel *shall* come to thee, O Israel!"

Extended note: The seven oracles as epochs of church history

It is common for proponents of both the historicist and futurist approaches to interpret the seven oracles as seven sequential epochs of church history. This has the advantage of allowing the interpreter to account for the distance between John's setting and the alleged fulfillment of the events recounted in the visions beginning in chapter 4, and is especially important in this regard in futurist interpretations. Such readings, however, exhibit a Eurocentric and, more particularly, Protestant-centered reading quite starkly. The focus of attention moves from the apostolic age (Ephesus), through the period of persecutions from Nero through Diocletian and Maximian (Smyrna), and through the period of legalization under Constantine (Pergamum). At this point the Western church moves onto center stage to the exclusion of Christianity elsewhere. The oracle to Thyatira characterizes (caricatures) the period of the papacy, the oracle to Sardis speaks of the Western post-Enlightenment church, the oracle to Philadelphia the Great Awakening and missionary endeavors of England and the United States, and, finally, Laodicea the lukewarm state of the modern church (again, in the West).

Aside from the gross oversimplification this imposes even upon the Western church, the scheme completely neglects the state of the church in the southern hemisphere and the Middle and Far East. The scheme presumes that God, in revealing this information, is really only concerned with the Western church up through the Reformation, and thereafter with the

Protestant churches, largely in Great Britain and America. If the oracle to Laodicea is meant to characterize the church of the present day, the glorified Christ would be giving no notice to the millions of faithful Christians in the developing world whose fidelity to God under great pressure, and whose enthusiasm for evangelism, far more closely resemble the conditions in Smyrna and Philadelphia than Laodicea.

Regarding each church as representative of the whole church in a particular era grossly caricatures the periods of church history so described. Moreover, there has never been an era in which the diversity of the churches addressed by Revelation—and greater diversity besides—failed to be represented. I find it more prudent to regard the seven churches together as typical of the kinds of congregations one might find throughout the world in any and every age, rather than each one as typical of the entire church in any one period.

Optional Exercise: *The section "Listening for what the Spirit is saying to the churches" begins with a series of questions based on the pattern found in the seven oracles. (1) Use these questions as an agenda for prayerful discernment and discussion in the setting of a group in your church (a staff meeting, a Bible study group, an administrative committee, etc.). (2) Use these questions as an agenda for reflection on a particular biblical passage outside of Revelation (for example, a passage from the prophets, the teachings of Jesus, or an Epistle). These questions may be used both for self-examination and for prayerful reflection on your faith community in light of that passage.*

Chapter 5

JOHN'S PROCLAMATION OF THE ONE WHO IS, WHO WAS, AND IS COMING

John writes to the seven congregations mindful of the well-established practice of testing prophetic utterances. He has himself commended the Ephesian Christians for their examination and rejection of "those who say they are apostles but are not, and you have found them to be liars" (Rev 2:3 CEB). One important test for evaluating a new revelation was discerning whether or not it aligned with hitherto-accepted revelation, whether the apostolic tradition (as in Gal 1:6–9 and 1 John 1:1–4; 4:1–3) or the Scriptures that the apostles themselves accepted, and on the basis of which they legitimate their own message through demonstrating its consonance with those Scriptures. It is to this larger tradition that John and other prophets remain accountable, by which their words are to be tested and either approved or rejected.

John's own prophetic word is not accepted merely because he claims to have "seen" and "heard" what he communicates, but because what he communicates coheres with the traditions of the Jewish Scriptures and the teachings of Jesus shared by John and his congregations. And the judgment on John must be that his own revelation of God's character, actions, and purposes is overwhelmingly consonant with the "rule of faith" he learned from his exposure to the breadth of the Jewish Scriptures. John gives fresh expression to the essential proclamation about God found in the Old Testament, reminding his congregations of God's character, God's just requirements of his creatures, God's patterns of intervention in human affairs, and God's purposes for creation. This becomes the framework within which he assesses—and calls his congregations to assess—the dynamics of the world around them and the most faithful response within their situation.

In this chapter, we will explore Revelation as a brilliant, creative work of theology—a proclamation about the One God known throughout the many streams of Old Testament tradition, brought together here into one kaleidoscopic presentation by John, whose work as preacher and prophet grows out of his rich understanding of the God of the Scriptures and the God of Jesus. John is not primarily a wild-eyed prophet: he is a *theologian*. He is a person who knows God—the full picture of the God of Israel and the God of Jesus—better than most people in the seven churches, and perhaps better than most people in any church.

The God who is alone worthy of worship

John forcefully proclaims the One God who is alone worthy of worship and that targets idolatry as a behavior supremely to be avoided. John speaks in unison with the Shema, the fundamental "creed" of Judaism recited twice daily by every pious Jew in the ancient world: "Hear, O Israel: The LORD is our God, the LORD alone" (Deut 6:4 NRSV). And the Shema is, indeed, a faith claim about the uniqueness of the God of Abraham, Isaac, and Jacob, and the unique right this God has to the loyal obedience of the people: "You shall love the LORD your God with all your heart, and with all your soul, and with all your might. Keep these words that I am commanding you today" (Deut 6:5–6 NRSV).

Foremost among those words are the opening commandments of the Decalogue, the Ten Commandments: "I am the LORD your God. . . . You shall have no other gods before me. You shall not make for yourself an idol, whether in the form of anything that is in heaven above, or that is on the earth beneath, or that is in the water under the earth. You shall not bow down to them or worship them" (Deut 5:6–9). The Hebrew Bible is full of commentary upon, and application of, this central summons. It is a theme that pervades historical books (e.g., 2 Kgs 17:9–18), wisdom literature and liturgical texts

(Ps 96:1–9; 97:6–7; 115:3–11; 135:13–21; Wis 13:1–15:17), and the prophetic writings (e.g., Isa 44:6–24; Jer 10:1–11). John's heart beats with this same pulse as he manifests his intense concern with "keeping the commandments of God" (Rev 12:17; 14:12), and the first and second commandments are foremost in his mind as he calls the churches away from "food sacrificed to idols" (Rev 2:14, 20) and from any compromise with idolatry (Rev 9:20–21), especially the imperial cult (Rev 13:1–18). John gives voice to the eternal call to "fear God and give him glory," to offer God worship as "the one who made heaven and earth and sea and springs of water" (Rev 14:6–7), rather than to offer worship to "the gods that did not make the heavens and the earth" (Jer 10:11; see also Ps 96:5).

John's proclamation calls his hearers to examine their own practices of "worship" closely. What do we worship besides God? What claims our allegiance ahead of God? What other things do we value enough that we hold back in our response to God's call or Jesus' directions? John particularly focuses on the danger, the lure, of idolatry. This was an ever-present reality in his setting, as it continues to be, for example, for the Christian minorities living in India or Sri Lanka, who are surrounded by sacred sites ancient and modern built around iconic representations of the divine. Christians in North America are not confronted with idolatry in its historic form, though there is much to be gained from examining the extent to which we are entangled in more sublimated forms of idolatry. Jesus hinted at this possibility even within the context of monotheistic, anti-iconic Judea and Galilee: "You cannot serve God and Mammon" (Matt 6:24), that is, wealth.

As we consider the breadth of John's own understanding of the God of Israel and the God of Jesus, perhaps it is well also to examine whether we are ourselves worshiping *God*, or to some extent worshiping more an *image* of God. In other words, while we are likely not in danger of making a carved image of God for use in worship, we may nevertheless have fallen prey to shaping a mental image of God and worshiping *this* god. The theologians of ancient Israel must have had significant insight into the problem of fashioning any image of the divine to steer the nation's practice so forcefully and so directly against the

near-universal tendency to create sculpted images as a means
of interacting with the divine. Perhaps that insight included
the realizations that no image captures the whole of the thing
represented (in this case, the whole of God) and that the (par-
tial) image inevitably replaces the reality. Encounter with the
divine is thereby not facilitated, in the end, but distorted and
interrupted.

John proclamation of God's character, interests, and interventions, rooted in so many streams of the scriptural tradition,
may challenge us in regard to our images of God. Is our image
of God as multifaceted, as complete, as John's? Or do we carry
about and worship a personal image of God, a favorite mental
picture of God, that has replaced the larger reality of who God
is? Some may worship only the God of love and acceptance
who makes no demands in terms of our holiness and commitment to justice. Some may worship a God of personal salvation
who seeks individual decisions, but who is not concerned about
fair access for all to what is necessary for a life of dignity. Still
others may worship the God who is available to them when
they want assurance that they're not alone or when they want
help or comfort in life's difficulties, but not the God to whom
they must keep themselves available, to serve and not simply
be served. One of John's often overlooked contributions to
Christian theology and the Christian practice that is shaped by
theology is his weaving together of so many different facets of
God, inviting us thereby to draw closer to the full reality.

The God who indicts domination systems

The label "domination system" has come to be applied
to systemic social arrangements that institutionalize unequal
power relationships and that use those power relationships in
the interest of the empowered, often to the detriment of the
less empowered or unempowered. Dominations systems are
the standard operating modes of societies that have ordered
themselves around the goals of securing the privilege of the
few, or the pursuit of wealth or power by the few, as the highest considerations. Such orderings of a society lead inevitably

to the disregard for the fair distribution of this world's goods and to disregard for the socially, politically, and economically vulnerable. These systems develop their own "logic" into which they typically indoctrinate all participants, so that ongoing commitment to the system is assured even by those who are most disadvantaged by the system. They are also often accompanied by ideologies of self-aggrandizement, if not self-worship, that also serve to mask the costs of the systems in terms of human suffering and dignity.

Examples of domination systems would include militarism, the willingness to kill (or that another person should be killed) in order that my own interests should be protected; capitalism (alongside other economic "isms"), the willingness for others to lose access even to a secure and stable livelihood in order that my own enjoyment of excess be protected; and environmental consumption, the willingness for future generations (and many present populations) to find themselves in an ecologically less secure position so that I can keep enjoying the profits and conveniences that I enjoy.[1]

John's indictment of Rome (Rev 17–18) is entirely in keeping with the Hebrew prophetic tradition in which God sets himself against any society that sets the pursuit of wealth or power as the highest consideration. This strain emerges throughout the major prophets, particularly in those texts upon which John draws (e.g., Isa 23; 47; Jer 51; Ezek 26–27). It is rooted in the Exodus event itself, when God took the side of an oppressed and enslaved people, at the cost of whose dehumanization the great treasure cities of Egypt were being constructed (the treasures of Egypt themselves often coming from violent conquest, enforced tribute, and economic rapine). The classical prophets did not only turn this critical eye to foreign

---

[1] Helpful introductions to domination systems, their rules of operation, and their effects include C. Dale White, *Making a Just Peace: Human Rights & Domination Systems* (Nashville: Abingdon, 1988); Walter Wink, *Naming the Powers* (Minneapolis: Fortress, 1983); Walter Wink, *Unmasking the Powers* (Minneapolis: Fortress, 1986); Walter Wink, *Engaging the Powers* (Minneapolis: Augsburg Fortress, 1992); Wes Howard-Brook and Anthony Gwyther, *Unveiling Empire: Reading Revelation Then and Now* (New York: Orbis, 1999).

powers, but also indicted Israel when it put the enjoyment of luxury by the few ahead of the survival of the many, or when it forgot the covenant loyalty due God, reveling instead in its alliances with other powers that allowed the elites to achieve greater economic growth or political influence.

From his close reading of the prophets, John has discerned what the response of the God of the prophets would be to a new, grander, more overtly self-deifying, and more violently expansive domination system. He brings those prophetic traditions to bear on the situation facing his congregations to help them see their context in light of those paradigms of violent oppression, luxurious over-consumption, and self-legitimating ideology.

John was not alone in presenting such a close correspondence between Roman domination and the prophetic critique of empire. The authors of *4 Ezra* and *2 Baruch* came to the same conclusion regarding Rome's status in the sight of the One God on the basis of their reading of the Hebrew scriptural tradition as well. The author of *4 Ezra* also talks about Rome in connection with the four beasts of Daniel 7 (*4 Ezra* 12:11–12), though somewhat differently from John as he makes Rome the fourth beast rather than a combination of all four. Nevertheless, he writes:

> You, the fourth beast that has come, have conquered all the beasts that have gone before; and you have held sway over the world with great terror, and over all the earth with grievous oppression; and for so long you have lived on the earth with deceit. You have judged the earth, but not with truth, for you have oppressed the meek and injured the peaceable; you have hated those who tell the truth, and have loved liars; you have destroyed the homes of those who brought forth fruit, and have laid low the walls of those who did you no harm. Your insolence has come up before the Most High, and your pride to the Mighty One. . . . Therefore you, eagle, will surely disappear, . . . so that the whole earth, freed from your violence, may be refreshed and relieved. (*4 Ezra* 11:40–46)

The charges of violence, oppression, deception, and pride are essentially the same (John will dwell more upon luxurious consumption, in addition) and suggest that deep immersion in the Hebrew scriptural tradition led two apocalypticists independently to one inescapable conclusion concerning the domination system of Roman imperialism.

John's proclamation of a God who opposes domination systems challenges hearers in every age to examine themselves and their practices lest they be found among those who profit from and are privileged by the same, and who will therefore receive their share in God's judgment of the same. Rather, Christ-followers are called to take up their stand alongside God, God's prophets like John, and Jesus himself against the practices that interfere with God's good vision for *all* people—those practices that safeguard the interests of *some* at the expense of *others*.

The God of the Exodus

The importance of the Exodus story for shaping the Jewish people's knowledge of God cannot be overestimated. Its centrality is evident from the opening words of the Decalogue: "I am the LORD your God, who brought you out of the land of Egypt, out of the house of slavery; you shall have no other gods before me" (Exod 20:2–3 NRSV; see also Deut 5:6–7). The Exodus story as a revelation of the character of God and God's interventions was held continually before the worshiping community in its Psalms (see, e.g., Pss 78, 105, 106) and canticles (e.g., the Song of Moses in Exod 15:1–18). Prophets regularly invoked the Exodus as the beneficent act on the basis of which the obligations of the covenant were grounded (e.g., Ezek 20:3–26) and as the precedent for the hope of a New Exodus from the Babylonian Captivity (as in Isa 40:3–5; 43:16–19; 52:1–6).

John stands in line with this tradition, proclaiming the One seated upon the throne as the God of the Exodus, who now works the final deliverance of God's people in a definitive Exodus. John draws his description of the Christian communities as "a kingdom and priests to our God" (Rev 5:10; cf. 1:5–6) from God's address to the Exodus generation, calling them to be "for me a priestly kingdom" (Exod 19:6). John shares in the Christian conviction that this priestly kingdom transcends ethnic identity, being constituted not merely by Jacob's de-scendants, but by people drawn from "every tribe and lan-guage and people and nation" (Rev 5:9 NRSV). The plagues that God visits upon the inhabitants of the earth in the seven trumpets and seven bowls recall, in many of their particulars, the plagues visited upon Egypt in Exodus 7:14–10:29. These include the return of plagues involving boils (Exod 9:10; Rev 16:2), water turning to blood (Exod 7:20–21; Rev 16:3–4), darkness (Exod 10:21; Rev 16:10), frogs (Exod 8:2–3; Rev 16:13), and hailstones (Exod 9:24; Rev 16:21). As in Exodus, the plagues are meant to induce repentance, though they are once again unsuccessful in this regard, as they were in Exodus (Exod 8:15, 19, 32, etc.; Rev 9:20–21; 16:9, 11, 21).

By drawing these correspondences, John may be seeking not so much to communicate about the specific ways in which God will punish a rebellious world, but rather to shape the hear-ers' understanding of the character of the world in which they are living. What does it say about the condition of the people of God under Roman rule that God should find it necessary to bring all the plagues of Egypt again upon the world? John depicts future consequences in order to communicate some-thing about present causes. Roman Asia Minor, and indeed Roman imperialism as a whole, imposes a state of oppression. The people of God need deliverance from that system; they do not need to seek avenues for cooperation with that system (as, for example, the rival teachers in Pergamum and Thyatira are urging). Indeed, partnership is impossible, for the parties in-volved are oppressive taskmasters and subjugated peoples who are not even permitted to worship as their God requires. At the same time, John is invoking the historical precedent of the Exodus to assure Christ-followers that God is indeed deeply concerned with the plight of God's people and will intervene for their liberation from the domination systems of the world.

As in Exodus, the people of God are sealed for protection from the plagues (Rev 7:1–8; 9:4; 16:2). The marking of the doorposts and lintels of the Hebrews' houses with the blood of the (Passover) lamb is the most striking image associated therewith, but God's protection was evident also when the plagues did not affect the land, livestock, and human inhabitants of Goshen, where the Hebrews resided (Exod 8:22–23; 9:6–7, 25–26; 10:22–23). Perhaps it is significant that Moses' pretext for the Exodus was the need for his people to worship God beyond the borders of Egypt, since the Hebrews and Egyptians cherished mutually offensive religious practices (Exod 5:3; 7:16; 8:1, 20, 25–27; 9:13; 10:3, 7–11). In Revelation's New Exodus, worship remains a primary concern—one that again involves separation from the rites cherished by the oppressor (e.g., Rev 13:11–18; 14:9–11). The redeemed finally sing of God's deliverance by the side of a new sea (Rev 15:2–4), with the song of Moses now linked with the song of the Lamb. The Exodus, seen also through the tradition of the new Exodus of Isaiah in which the faithful are brought out of Babylon (cf. Rev 18:4–8) and into a new land of promise (Rev 21:1–22:5), becomes the framework within which to speak of a much grander deliverance.

If John successfully broadens our image of God to make room for the God of the Exodus, it follows that our practice of following a God whose character includes such concerns must be broadened correspondingly. And so we might examine ourselves: To what extent are we in touch with the many in this world who desperately need such deliverance from oppression? Have we, like Moses, left Pharaoh's courts and palaces to see the plight of God's people beyond our places of comfort? Have we, like Moses, turned against "our own" in the spaces of privilege because we are so grieved at the plight of the exploited, the oppressed, the people consigned to poverty or starvation, the people thrown in prison because they threaten the privileged? Have we the faith of Moses and of John in the God of the Exodus, such that we choose oppression alongside God's people in Goshen, rather than continue to carry on pleasantly in Egypt in ignorance or apathy?

The God who vindicates God's faithful ones

The psalmists expressed confidence in God's commitment not only to deliver God's people collectively when they fell into distress or oppression, but also to deliver each faithful one from his or her distress: "Many are the afflictions of the righteous, but the LORD rescues them from them all" (Ps 34:19 NRSV). The underlying rationale for such bold confidence derives ultimately from Deuteronomy, which promised that covenant loyalty would result in the safe enjoyment of the land and, when that was threatened, God's aid. This promise is echoed throughout the wisdom tradition (e.g., Prov 3:1–11) and in the Psalms as well.

In seasons of distress, whether from natural calamity or hostile aggression, the faithful would wait expectantly for God's intervention. Their knowledge that they had walked in line with God's commandments (often coupled with the suspicion that their enemies did not) gave them the grounds for expecting deliverance. Since God was just, God would necessarily intervene to bring the promised blessings to the righteous and just punishment to the wicked. If the ungodly gained ascendancy over the righteous person, the cry went up for vindication:

> How long, O LORD? Will you forget me forever? How long will you hide your face from me? How long must I bear pain in my soul, and have sorrow in my heart all day long? How long shall my enemy be exalted over me? (Ps 13:1–2 NRSV)

The just God could not allow the wicked to put the righteous person to shame and to gain honor or profit at the expense of the godly or the weak (see Pss 35:24–26; 94:1–6). This same conviction found expression in regard to the fortunes of the nation as well: the cry for vindication can go up on behalf of the slain and oppressed of the entire nation (as in Ps 79).

In the events prior to the Maccabean Revolt, pious Jews were being martyred under the Greco-Syrian king Antiochus IV and his renegade Jewish deputies (see 2 Macc 6–7), often in a degrading and painful manner, explicitly because of their refusal to break faith with the covenant God. In this context, the expectation arose that the righteous person's commitment to God would be vindicated after death. The righteous would be rewarded with the covenant blessings in the life beyond death, and their lawless persecutors would be punished and made to acknowledge the nobility and wisdom of the righteous ones whom they mocked and killed (see 2 Macc 7:9, 11, 14,

17, 19, 23, 31, 35–36; 4 Macc 9:8–9, 32; 10:11, 15; 12:11–12; 17:4–6; Wis 1:16–5:23).

When John depicts the souls of the righteous, slain for the sake of God's word, crying out for vindication (Rev 6:9–11), he stands in line with this tradition, confessing the justice of God and, therefore, the expectation of God's intervention to uphold the cause of the righteous. He stands firmly in the tradition that claims that even death is insufficient to thwart God's commitment to give justice to those who had walked faithfully in line with God's commandments: "How long, holy and true Sovereign, will you not give judgment and require our blood from the inhabitants of the earth?!" (Rev 6:10). As the narrative unfolds, John affirms the truthfulness of the tradition's foundational premises: God is indeed just in all God's ways (Rev 15:2–4), as will be seen when God dramatically avenges the blood of God's holy ones: "You are just, You who are and were, the Holy One, because you have rendered these judgments, because they poured out the blood of holy ones and prophets, and you have given them blood to drink, for they deserve it" (Rev 16:5–6). The martyrs themselves confirm God's justice, adding their "Amen" from beneath the altar to the angel's declaration (Rev 16:7). The scenes of God's judgment throughout Revelation are anchored in this traditional expectation that God vindicates God's servants, an expectation relevant to the past and forthcoming violence against the Christian communities (Rev 2:10, 13; 6:9–11; 11:18; 13:15–17; 17:6; 18:24).

When we read texts that speak about God's vindication of God's own, we may tend to think first about the ways in which we may feel that we need vindication by God to some degree. Perhaps this facet of the God proclaimed by John calls us to think and look again beyond ourselves to sisters and brothers in much greater need of vindication, since they suffer significant loss and disgrace for their commitment to stand alongside Christ in their contexts. In my own context at Ashland Theological Seminary, thanks in large measure to colleagues who are committed to the global church and to raising awareness about the needs of the same, and in part to personal connections abroad, I hear regularly about the plight of Christians whose contexts are unsupportive of their religious commitments at best, and explicitly intolerant and repressive at worst. If our God is the God who will vindicate *them*, how should that lead us, as servants of God, to include them in our care? To find ways to stand alongside them, encourage them, lobby *here* to raise awareness of and perhaps even foster intervention in their predicament? To be their family in deed through our investment in them, and not merely their family in word?

The God who exercises sovereign rule over the cosmos

John proclaims God as the *Pantokratōr* (Rev 15:3), the One who holds all things within his grasp. This God appears consistently as One sitting enthroned (Rev 4:2, 9, 10; 5:1, 7, 13; 6:16, etc.), a posture that declares God's reign over the cosmos. Once again, Revelation is entirely consonant with the witness of the scriptural traditions, particularly the Psalms, which keep God's rule in the forefront of the worshipers' consciousness.

> "The Lord is king. . . . Your throne is established from of old." (Ps 93:1–2 NRSV)

> "The Lord is king." (Ps 97:1; 99:1 NRSV)

God sits in heavenly session, presiding over a court populated by supernatural beings who stand and wait to do God's bidding and pay God homage as sovereign:

> Bless the Lord, O you his angels, you mighty ones who do his bidding, obedient to his spoken word. Bless the Lord, all his hosts, his ministers that do his will. (Ps 103:20–21 NRSV)

> Praise him, all his angels; praise him, all his host! (Ps 148:2 NRSV)

> Blessed are you in the temple of your holy glory, . . . who look into the depths from your throne on the cherubim. (Sg Three 31–32 NRSV)

Songs such as the last one were inspired by the physical representations of God in the temple, where God sits enthroned invisibly above the ark of the covenant, the top of which is decorated with the two cherubim that uphold God's throne, God's "seat." Visionaries like Isaiah elaborate upon this, providing visions of God upon this throne, surrounded by multiple angelic beings offering ceaseless worship (Isa 6:1–6). Ezekiel gives a rather different, more daringly detailed, and more colorful depiction of the same (Ezek 1:4–28). The author of *Testament of Levi*, a Jewish text from the first century B.C.E., elaborates still more upon this foundation, providing a vision of God enthroned in the highest heaven, surrounded by several distinct orders of angels performing different functions within the heavenly court, all visually expressive of God's rule over the cosmos. John's vision of the enthroned One, and of the activity of the orders of heavenly beings around the throne, stands firmly in line with this tradition.

The Hebrew Scriptures consistently affirm that God's sovereign rule brings justice to human affairs. The liturgical traditions of Israel particularly emphasize God's reign in judgment, judging the earth, the nations, and their peoples:

> He will judge the peoples with equity. . . . He will judge the world with righteousness, and the peoples with his truth. (Ps 96:10, 13 NRSV)

> Righteousness and justice are the foundation of his throne. (Ps 97:2 NRSV)

> He is coming to judge . . . the world with righteousness, and the peoples with equity. (Ps 98:9)

> The LORD is king. . . . He sits enthroned upon the cherubim. . . . Mighty King, lover of justice, you have established equity; you have executed justice. (Ps 99:1, 4 NRSV)

John also foregrounds this particular aspect of God's rule. The "good news" about God's accession to the reins of the kingdoms of this world is the manifestation of God's justice in this human sphere:

> "We give thanks to you, Lord God Pantokrator, who is and who was, because you have taken up your great power and exercised sovereign rule. And the nations were enraged, and your wrath

came, and the right time to judge the dead, and to give the re-
ward to your slaves, to the prophets and the holy ones and those
fearing your name, the small and the great, and to ravage the
ravagers of the earth." (Rev 11:16–18)

"Alleluia! The deliverance and the glory and the power of our
God! Because he judged the great Prostitute, who ravaged the
earth in her fornication, and he required the blood of his slaves
from her hand. . . . Alleluia! Because the Lord God, the Pan-
tokrator, exercised sovereign rule." (Rev 19:1–2, 6)

God's exercise of punitive judgment makes way for a new order
of human community, as the latter hymn goes on to celebrate
the coming marriage feast of the Lamb, which leads in turn to
the vision of the New Jerusalem, a multinational human community "done right."

Worship of the One seated upon the throne is, of course, a
spiritual practice that invites us to examine our lives for signs of
reflecting the reality of God's rule, or, alternatively, the rule of
self-determination and looking out for our own interests rather
than God's interests. But since the coming of God's kingdom
means also the breaking in of God's justice throughout this
world, John would challenge us to examine our alignment here
in particular. Are we sufficiently in touch with the injustice
faced by our sisters and brothers *some*where in this world to
know from the heart what it really means to cry out "Your
kingdom come!" to God in prayer on their behalf? In what
ways do we put ourselves at God's disposal, for God to use us
as agents and instruments for advancing the cause of his kingdom—his justice—in their situation? John's vision of elites and
merchants lamenting, but heaven rejoicing at God's judgment
of the domination systems of Rome, radically challenges us to
examine our own alignment with the perpetrators or with the
victims of injustice and oppression in this world.

The God who promises *shalom* in God's presence

God's reign moves toward establishing the order in the
natural and human spheres that reflects God's just character

and God's designs for human community in relationship with the divine. In Revelation, this finds its full expression in the vision of the New Jerusalem, where God's promises to God's people and, indeed, to the nations are finally brought to their full realization.

The image of this consummation as the wedding of God and God's people was poignantly expressed by the prophet Hosea (see Hos 2:14–20), whose own actions toward his wayward wife, Gomer, became a living parable of God's intentions toward Israel. Isaiah applies this image more particularly to Jerusalem as the bride of God in the context of God's vindication of the fortunes of God's people:

> The LORD delights in you, and your land shall be married. For as a young man marries a young woman, so shall your builder marry you, and as the bridegroom rejoices over the bride, so shall your God rejoice over you. (Isa 62:4–5 NRSV)

The tradition of the covenant as a wedding or marriage comes to expression in early Christian thought as the wedding of Christ (the "son") to the people of God, with the eschatological age being depicted as a wedding banquet. This has strong roots in the Jesus tradition (Matt 22:1–14 and parallels) and blends with the tradition of Zion/Jerusalem as God's bride in John's visions of "the holy city, New Jerusalem . . . descending out of heaven from God, prepared as a bride adorned for her husband" (Rev 21:2; see also Rev 19:6b–9; 21:9; 22:17).

The very idea of the "new heavens and new earth," together with the passing away of the "former things" and the re-creation of Jerusalem, reprises the hope expressed by Isaiah (Isa 65:17–18). When John represents the speech of "a great voice from the throne" announcing this great consummation, he speaks entirely in the language of the prophets who had previously communicated this hope:

> Look—the tent of God is with humankind, and he will make his home with them, and they will be his people, and God himself will be with them, and he will wipe away every tear from their eyes, and death will no longer be, nor grief, nor crying, neither will there be suffering, because the former things passed away. (Rev 21:3–4)

Several promises previously articulated in God's name would be recognizable: "I will dwell in your midst" (Zech 2:11 NRSV); "I will walk among you, and will be your God, and you shall be my people" (Lev 26:12 NRSV); "Then they shall be my people, and I will be their God" (Ezek 11:20 NRSV); "My dwelling place shall be with them; and I will be their God, and they shall be my people" (Ezek 37:27 NRSV); "Then the Lord GOD will wipe away the tears from all faces" (Isa 25:8 NRSV); "No more shall the sound of weeping be heard in it [Jerusalem], or the cry of distress" (Isa 65:19 NRSV). In the promise to "the one who overcomes" that immediately follows in Rev 21:7, namely, that "I will be to him or her a God, and he or she will be to me a son or a daughter," the hearers encounter the familiar promise from 2 Sam 7:14, applied first to the Davidic dynasty, then to the Messiah, and here extended to the whole of the Christian community in keeping with the theme of the "people of the holy ones" sharing in the rule of God's Anointed. God's promises will not fail. God *will* usher in a fully restored community.

John differs from his sources in two significant particulars. The first of these concerns the scope of God's promises, which for John includes men and women from every tribe, and language group, and people, and nation (5:9–10; 7:9; 14:6–7), rather than reflecting God's particular investment in the one ethnic people of Israel. This is in keeping, of course, with some prophetic voices (like those heard in Isa 60:3–5 and Zech 2:11–12) against others (like Ezekiel's in 37:27–28), but stands all the more in line with major streams of early Christian interpretation of the Hebrew scriptural hope (e.g., Luke 3:1–6; Acts 10–11, 15; Rom 15:7–13; Gal 3:1–4:7; Eph 3:1–6; 1 Pet 2:4–10).

The second point of divergence is more pronounced, namely, the emphatic absence of a temple in the New Jerusalem. This contrasts starkly with Ezekiel, who devotes nine chapters to describing how the perfect temple would be constructed (Ezek 40–48). This divergence is all the more striking given the other similarities between John's vision and Ezekiel's vision of the new or restored Jerusalem, both involving an angelic being with a measuring rod ushering the seer around the complex and exploring every gate, wall, and structure. John, however, has a clear rationale for this difference (21:22): the full presence of God and the Lamb in this city eliminate the need for a temple, since the limits on access to God implied by the temple structure (see Heb 9:1–8) have been completely transcended in God's perfect future.

These visions communicate something about God's ultimate purposes for human community, and thus invite us to examine ourselves in terms of our investment in cooperating with those purposes. How do we make room for God's *shalom* to break into our world? How do we create room for God to draw near to people from every nation and language group, and for people from every nation and language group to draw near to God and to one another in reconciliation and in mutual investment in the other's wholeness? Where do we work to create spaces and "alternative communities" where Babylon's agenda, values, and power do not dominate—seeking to form at least temporary experiences of community built around Jesus' and the apostles' vision for (and *commands* to bring about) an alternative way of living together?

The God whose patience has an end

It is not John's visions of cosmic renewal and healing that elicit criticism of his voice, but rather his claims about certain groups of people being cast into the lake of fire or barred from entering the New Jerusalem because they chose a different path than he advises. These were the visions that set D. H. Lawrence on edge, as he condemned John for betraying the New Testament vision of love with his "lake of burning brimstone in which devils, demons, beasts, and bad men should frizzle and suffer for ever and ever and ever, Amen!"[2] These are the claims that continue to evoke accusations of bullying audiences into submitting to his authority among modern scholars. The framers of the Revised Common Lectionary could not even permit one verse from Revelation speaking of exclusion alongside

---

[2] D. H. Lawrence, *Apocalypse* (New York: A. A. Knopf, 1931), 117.

inclusion, omitting 22:15 from the reading of 22:12–21 on the seventh Sunday of Easter—ironically also eliminating the reading of those verses that warn against the strategic omission of such problematic verses (22:18–19).

And yet, even in Revelation's most objectionable parts, those words that rub most gratingly against our cultural values of tolerance and pluralism, even here John does no more than speak in line with the tradition of which he has become the curator and spokesperson. When he proclaims a God who, having created a just kingdom, excludes, punishes, or destroys that which is unjust, rebellious, and not aligned with God, he faithfully portrays that "other side" of God that shows through the Torah, the former and later prophets, and, ultimately, Jesus himself.

In Isaiah's celebration of the New Exodus that God would make for God's people, the prophet includes a note of exclusivity concerning God's new highway through the desert: "The unclean shall not travel on it" (Isa 35:8 NRSV). When the same prophet describes the renewed Jerusalem, he calls Zion to rejoice in part because "the uncircumcised and the unclean shall enter you no more" (Isa 52:1 NRSV). In Ezekiel, immediately following the promise that "they shall be my people, and I will be their God" (Ezek 11:20 NRSV), God turns his attention to those "whose heart goes after their detestable things and their abominations," who will be excluded from the renewed Jerusalem (Ezek 11:21 NRSV).

In keeping with their awareness that God's city and restored temple precincts are holy, these authors all speak of the exclusion of those who are polluted. John's vision of the "holy city" in which God dwells in all of God's fullness, therefore, quite naturally invites similar discussion of classes of pollution that disqualify one from approaching the Holy One in the holy places of God's dwelling. John's lists (Rev 21:8, 27; 22:15) are notable insofar as they involve not ritual pollution but moral failure, particularly the failure to take a courageous and loyal stand by God and God's Christ. In this manner, they align with the broadening of the scope of God's salvation to members of every nation (John does not exclude "the uncircumcised" as such, as do Isaiah and Ezekiel).

Above all, John's proclamation of a God who holds rebellious humanity accountable for their affronts against God's honor and rightful claim to obedience resonates with the sayings of Jesus. Matthew 13:41–43 is a case in point: "The Son of Man will send his angels, and they will gather together out of his kingdom all the stumbling blocks and those practicing unlawfulness and 'will throw them into the fiery furnace' [see Dan 3:6]: weeping and gnashing of teeth shall be there. Then the righteous will shine like the sun in the kingdom of their Father. Let the one with ears listen." Jesus' exclusion of "the stumbling blocks and those practicing unlawfulness" from the kingdom of the Son of Man corresponds quite closely with Rev 21:8, 27; 22:15. John simply defines more precisely what constitutes a stumbling block or unlawfulness in his pastoral situation.

Furthermore, Jesus describes the place of exclusion in terms suggesting severe pain and torment: "they 'will throw them into the furnace of fire'," where there will be "weeping and gnashing of teeth," a detail not suggestive of quick incineration (Matt 13:42). Revelation 14:9–11 elaborates this image of judgment by the Messiah, again with specific infractions identified, very much in line with the first commandments of the Decalogue, the prohibitions against worshiping other gods and making cult images for worship.

At the close of Jesus' "Apocalyptic Discourse" in Matthew, perhaps the most vivid description of the "Last Judgment," the Son of Man sends away those who have failed to return gratitude to him in the persons of the hungry, naked, homeless, and imprisoned, to a place of endless torment—the "eternal fire prepared for the devil and his angels" (Matt 25:41 NRSV). This closely resembles the "lake of fire" in Revelation, also populated by both Satan, his minions, and those human beings deceived by him (Rev 14:9–11; 19:20; 20:10, 14–15). John is not, in these regards, more exclusive or vindictive than Jesus (at least as the latter is represented in the traditions attributed to him in the Gospels).

The question here is not whether John's vision is profoundly disturbing, but whether John is fairly representing and applying the traditions of the Jewish Scriptures, Jesus, and the early church—or giving expression to violence, hatred, or venom in a manner that betrays the tradition. And, in light of John's alignment with the Hebrew Scriptures, Jesus tradition, and apostolic tradition in so many points, it is also hardly the case that John is merely trying to get the hearers to accept "his" views.

John faithfully portrays a facet of God that many find distasteful, a facet that, though reflected throughout the Scriptures of both testaments, many exclude from the image of the God they worship. Nevertheless, John's proclamation challenges us to ask, if we are to worship the God known in the whole counsel of Scripture, whether we might stand in need of recovering a reasonable fear of God, a healthy respect for God's justice and God's power that will keep a fire kindled within us to get in line with God's agenda sooner rather than later, more rather than less, to the degree that God merits rather than to the degree we can comfortably accommodate. John's emphasis on judgment—and that primarily in terms of what we have *done* rather than what we have *believed*—challenges us to examine whether we are really hearing and heeding the words of Jesus when he said, "What's the use of calling me 'Lord' if you don't do what I tell you?"

Conclusion

John's closing vision presents human society organized with God—God's reign, God's light, God's justice—at the center of all things. John has never seen anything like this in life, not in Rome, not in Ephesus, not even in Jerusalem. New Jerusalem is not "brought about by famine and war and pestilence and natural disaster."[3] It is prepared as the people of God engage the acts of justice and righteousness that spin the fine linen in which the bride is robed. It is built on the foundations of the apostles (Rev 21:14), not on the foundations of violence or greed, but on the gospel of the truth of God. The new city

---

[3] Against the claim made by Tina Pippin, *Death and Desire: The Rhetoric of Gender in the Apocalypse of John* (Louisville: Westminster John Knox, 1992), 102–3.

exists to bring peace and healing to the nations (Rev 22:2), rather than to establish "peace" by controlling, dominating, and subduing. The city faces no threat (the gates are never shut, Rev 21:25). Military conquest, international strife, struggles for maintaining a balance of power, are all done away with in this vision. Resources are expended no longer in futile wars and power struggles but rather for the well-being of all. In the end, only God and God's Anointed can usher in the consummate reign of God. All we can do is *witness* to that reign by speaking and living together in ways aligned now with God's reign.

New Jerusalem is a costly alternative. One cannot profit from Babylon's partnership and violence and expect a welcome in the New Jerusalem (Rev 21:8, 27). We cannot legitimate our society's failure to enact God's righteousness, however this failure manifests itself, either by our participation or our silence. John urges disciples to learn how to live as aliens in a land that is not our own, looking away to our native land, the city that none of us has yet seen but that is the consummation of the great story of God.

> Now, in the meanwhile, with hearts raised on high,
> We for that country must yearn and must sigh;
> Seeking Jerusalem, dear native land,
> Through our long exile on Babylon's strand.[4]

Even so, come, Lord Jesus.

Questions for Reflection and Discussion: Each of the seven sections in this chapter ends with a set of questions calling for examination of how we think about God. Take some time to think through these sets of questions, particularly with a view to identifying those facets of God that have not been cut deeply into your own God-image and the implications for your life of serving the God who possesses those qualities, interests, and commitments. Some find it helpful to write down such reflections in a journal for later review, expansion, and accountability. Use these questions also as a basis for discussion in a study group, if you are part of one.

---

[4]This is a verse from the twelfth-century hymn, *O quanta qualia sunt illa Sabbata*, written by Peter Abelard as translated from Latin into English by John M. Neale (*The Hymnal Noted*, 1854).

FOR FURTHER READING

Carey, Greg. *Ultimate Things: An Introduction to Jewish and Christian Apocalyptic Literature*. St. Louis: Chalice, 2005. A fine introduction to the apocalyptic genre and mind-set and to the larger body of literature that constitutes this genre.

deSilva, D. A. *Seeing Things John's Way: The Rhetoric of the Book of Revelation*. Louisville: Westminster John Knox Press, 2009. The in-depth scholarly work upon which the present volume was based. Chapters 1–4 and chapter 12 would be especially helpful for those wishing to immerse themselves further in the topics covered in this book.

Hemer, Colin J. *The Letters to the Seven Churches of Asia in their Local Setting*. England: JSOT Press, 1986. A now classic study of the historical settings of the seven churches and the impact of local knowledge on the interpretation of Revelation.

Howard-Brook, Wes, and Anthony Gwyther. *Unveiling Empire: Reading Revelation Then and Now*. New York: Orbis, 1999. A reading of Revelation as a challenge to political and economic domination systems, ancient and modern.

Keener, Craig. *Revelation*. New International Version Application Commentary. Grand Rapids: Zondervan, 2000. An accessible commentary by a leading evangelical scholar, particularly interested in bridging the horizons between John's setting and our own.

Koester, Craig. *Revelation and the End of All Things*. Grand Rapids: Eerdmans, 2001. A fine discussion of the role of Revelation in Christian eschatology as well as a mini-commentary on Revelation itself, read from a historical perspective.

Kraybill, Nelson. *Apocalypse and Allegiance: Worship, Politics, and Devotion in the Book of Revelation*. Grand Rapids: Brazos, 2010. An excellent introduction to the Roman imperial context of Revelation, particular in its political and economic aspects.

Mounce, Robert H. *The Book of Revelation*. New International Commentary on the New Testament. Grand Rapids: Eerdmans, 1997. A solid commentary on Revelation for pastors and teachers.

Ramsey, W. M. *The Letters to the Seven Churches of Asia*. New York: Hodder & Stoughton, 1909. A classical study of the social and historical context of Revelation by a well-traveled scholar.

White, C. Dale. *Making a Just Peace: Human Rights & Domination Systems*. Nashville: Abingdon, 1998. An excellent primer on the ways in which systems take on an oppressive life of their own and enlist the unwitting support and acceptance of human participants.

Wilson, Mark. *Revelation*. Zondervan Illustrated Bible Backgrounds Commentary. Grand Rapids: Zondervan, 2007. A lavishly illustrated introduction to the archaeological, geographical, and cultural world of Roman Asia Minor and reading Revelation in its historical context.

Witherington, Ben, III. *Revelation*. Cambridge: Cambridge University Press, 2003. An accessible commentary on Revelation by a leading New Testament scholar.

INDEX OF ANCIENT SOURCES